TO IMPROVE
554
TIPS
YOUR PARTNER'S GAME

A TREASURY
OF BIDDING TIPS

EDDIE KANTAR
2ND ED. REVISED & UPDATED

MASTER POINT PRESS · TORONTO

Master Point Press
331 Douglas Ave.
Toronto, Ontario, Canada, M5M 1H2
(416)781-0351
Email: info@masterpointpress.com

Websites: www.masterpointpress.com
            www.teachbridge.com
            www.bridgeblogging.com
            www.ebooksbridge.com

Library and Archives Canada Cataloguing in Publication

Kantar, Edwin B., 1932-
      A treasury of bidding tips : 554 tips to improve your partner's bridge / Eddie Kantar. -- 2nd ed., rev. and updated.

Issued also in electronic format.
ISBN 978-1-897106-90-7

      1. Contract bridge--Bidding. I. Title.

GV1282.4.K362 2013   795.41'52   C2013-900124-7

Editor   Ray Lee
Copyediting/Interior format   Sally Sparrow
Cover and interior design   Olena S. Sullivan/New Mediatrix

1 2 3 4 5 6 7   17 16 15 14 13

PRINTED IN CANADA

To bid or not to bid, that is the question.
'Tis nobler to pass,' was Eddie's suggestion.
To preempt perchance, maybe to double
'Both of those calls,' he said, 'will spell trouble.'
I ran down the list of the bids that I knew
And Eddie admitted I knew quite a few.
The problem was clearly just evaluation,
Choosing the right bid for each situation.
How often a novice and even a master
Will suffer the slings of a bidding disaster.
That's why, I must tell you, this book is a pleasure.
The bidding tips herein I view as a treasure.
And I have not a doubt, long before the last page
You'll know just why Kantar's my favorite bridge sage!

Phyllis Fein (1991)

Contents

Introduction

The book you are holding is not meant for beginners, nor is it aimed at experts. It is directed at players somewhere between who would like to improve their game substantially. Could this be you? Let it be said at Trick 1 that few of these tips apply 100% of the time. Bidding tips seldom do. You must factor in variables such as the strength of your opponents, the strength of your partner, the strength of the intermediate cards in your long suit and the vulnerability, etc. However, an average player (your partner) should be able to improve his or her game considerably by following these tips. The reader is going to have to put a certain amount of trust (some would call it blind faith) in me. Most of these tips, a few of which are controversial, come with examples but not always with every supporting reason. If every reason were listed, you would be clutching a tome. An asterisk preceding a tip means that it is a controversial tip — that is, that some, however misguided, may not see it in exactly the same light as I do. Nonetheless, I stand by my asterisks! Actually it means that there is more than one way to play the sequence in question. I favor the method described, but the others have merit.

A 'must do' is to be aware of the chapter title in which a tip appears. For example, if the chapter is entitled, 'When You Are a Passed Hand,' those words will not appear before every tip. You must add them mentally to the tip for it to make sense. In the interest of brevity, certain abbreviations are used. The '+' means 'or more.' 10+ to 12 HCP means a 'good' 10 with strong intermediates for notrump evaluation. For suit evaluation, a + means no wasted strength such as jacks and queens in suits bid by the opponents, or perhaps a king or an AQ favorably located given the bidding. Thus, '11+ HCP' means '11 or more high-card points.' 'Strong suit' refers to any suit headed by at least three of the top five honors, the kind of suits your opponents hold. It might be wise to take these tips in small doses and try to absorb the messages; that is not to say that you should accept every tip or idea presented. If you play a different system and are comfortable with it, by all means disregard the tip. If it isn't broken, don't fix it.

Finally, I would like to thank Ron Garber, Norm Cressy and Allan Falk for looking over the original manuscript (including inserting and deleting some 1,000 commas) thus making my sentences intelligible. I also want to thank Jacqui DeRouin: without her sense of humor and computer expertise this book would never have seen the light of day. Finally, I have updated this edition mainly to include some new bidding ideas that have been introduced since the last edition.

Eddie Kantar

THE OPENING BID

1. Before opening the bidding with a distributional hand, prepare for various responses. Assume partner will respond in your shortest suit... he always does.

2. Deduct one point for any singleton jack, queen or king, as well as QJ doubleton. If you still have 12 points, open, otherwise, pass.

*3. With two five-card suits, open the bidding in the higher-ranking suit regardless of relative suit strength. However, with five clubs and five spades, open 1♣ if: (1) The hand is strong enough to jump shift; (2) The hand is minimum and the spades emaciated.

  a) ♠A4 ♡J8765 ◇AKJ87 ♣2
  b) ♠AKJ94 ♡43 ◇2 ♣AKQJ4
  c) ♠J8732 ♡A2 ◇2 ♣AK1087
  d) ♠AQ987 ♡32 ◇2 ♣AQ1043

With (a), open 1♡, the higher-ranking suit.
  With (b), open 1♣; you are strong enough to jump shift.
  With (c), open 1♣; the hand is minimum and the spades weak.
  With (d), open 1♠; the hand is minimum, but the spades are strong.

*4. With 4-4 in the minors, open the stronger suit — partner may wind up on lead. If the suits are of near equal strength, open 1◇.

  a) ♠A4 ♡J54 ◇KQJ9 ♣Q876
  b) ♠A4 ♡J54 ◇Q876 ♣KQJ9
  c) ♠A3 ♡J54 ◇QJ104 ♣AJ72

With (a), open 1◇. With (b), open 1♣. With (c), open 1◇.

*5. A short diamond is opened with one hand pattern: 4-4-3-2. In addition, the hand must be either too weak or too strong to open 1NT.

As dealer, you hold:

    a) ♠ A Q 5 4 ♡ A Q 5 4 ◇ J 5 4 ♣ 3 2

    b) ♠ A Q 5 4 ♡ A Q 5 4 ◇ A 8 7 ♣ 9 8

With (a), open 1 ◇. With (b), open 1NT.

6.   Do not open the bidding 1♣ holding only one or two clubs! 'Short club' does not mean this short!

*7.   With 4-3-3-3 distribution (the four-card suit a major) and a hand either too weak or too strong to open 1NT, open 1♣, not 1◇. (See Tip 5.)
    You hold:

♠ A J 8 ♡ K Q 8 7 ◇ A K J ♣ J 8 7

Open 1♣.

8.   It is permissible to open 1NT or 2NT with a small doubleton; however, do yourself a favor and at least have the other three suits stopped.

9.   With four clubs and four spades, and a hand strong enough to open 1NT but no stopper in either red suit, open 1♣.
    You hold:

♠ A K J 4 ♡ 3 2 ◇ 8 7 6 ♣ A K J 4

Open 1♣.

10.   With four diamonds and four spades, and a hand strong enough to open 1NT but no stopper in either clubs or hearts, open 1◇.
    You hold:

♠ A K Q 4 ♡ 6 5 4 ◇ A Q J 8 ♣ 4 2

Open 1◇. If partner responds 1♡, bid 1♠. If partner responds 2♣, bid 2♠.

*11.   With a balanced hand containing five hearts and 15-16 HCP, open 1NT. With 17 HCP, open 1♡.
    You hold:

a)	♠A 4 ♡K J 8 7 6 ◇A J 7 ♣Q 10 8
b)	♠A 4 ♡K J 9 8 7 ◇A Q 9 ♣K 10 6

With (a), open 1NT. If you open 1♡ and partner responds 1♠ or1NT, you have a rebid problem.

With (b), open 1♡. If partner responds 1♠, jump to 2NT. If partner responds 1NT, raise to 2NT. If partner responds 2♠ or 2◇, jump to 3NT. A 17-point hand with a five-card suit headed by any two honor cards should be treated as an 18-point hand.

*12. With a balanced hand containing five spades and 15-16 HCP, open 1♠ unless the spades are weak (zero or one honor card). If they are, open 1NT. With 17 HCP, open 1♠.

a)	♠J 7 6 5 4 ♡A J 9 ◇K J 10 ♣A Q
b)	♠K Q 8 7 6 ♡A 10 ◇A J 9 ♣Q 9 8

With (a), open 1NT. The spades are sick and you want the lead coming up to your hand.

With (b), open 1♠. The spades are strong and the wealth of intermediates actually make this more like a 17-point hand.

13. A five-card major should be no deterrent from opening 2NT (20-22 HCP).

*14. With 3=1=4=5 or 1=3=4=5 distribution, open 1◇ if the diamonds are strong, the clubs weak, and the hand has less than 17 HCP. The idea is to avoid rebidding 1NT with a small singleton in partner's suit.

a)	♠A 5 4 ♡3 ◇A Q J 9 ♣Q 8 7 6 5
b)	♠A 5 4 ♡3 ◇A Q J 9 ♣A Q 8 7 5
c)	♠A 5 4 ♡3 ◇K 9 3 2 ♣A Q J 8 7

With (a), open 1◇, avoiding a rebid problem if partner responds 1♡.

With (b), open 1♣; you are strong enough to reverse.

With (c), open 1♣; the clubs are strong enough to rebid.

15. With any 4-3-3-3 distribution, open with 13+ HCP; pass with 11 HCP or less. With exactly 12 HCP, open if your four-card suit is a minor. If your four-card suit is hearts or spades, meaning you have to open 1♣

with a three-card suit, you need intermediate spot cards to make up for that flaw.

a) ♠K J 8 ♡A 6 3 2 ◇K 4 3 ♣Q 3 2
b) ♠K J 8 4 ♡A 6 3 ◇Q 4 3 ♣Q 7 6
c) ♠K J 10 ♡A 10 3 2 ◇K 8 2 ♣J 10 4

With (a), open 1♣ with 13 HCP, no problem.

With (b), pass — 12 HCP, no intermediates, and you would have to open 1♣ with a three-card suit. (Two flaws.)

With (c), open 1♣. You have 12 HCP but you have good intermediates to take up the slack.

16. With any 4-4-3-2 distribution, open with 12+ HCP; pass with less.

a) ♠K J 8 4 ♡7 2 ◇A Q 5 4 ♣Q 4 3
b) ♠7 2 ♡K J 8 4 ◇Q 4 3 ♣A J 7 6

With (a), open 1 ◇. With (b), pass.

17. With any 4-4-4-1 pattern, open with 12+ HCP. Open 1◇ unless the singleton is in diamonds, then open 1♣.

18. With 4-4-4-1 distribution, deduct 1 point if the singleton is a jack, queen, or king.

a) ♠A Q 7 6 ♡3 ◇K J 5 4 ♣J 4 3 2
b) ♠A Q 7 6 ♡K 4 3 2 ◇K 10 7 6 ♣5

With (a), 11 HCP, pass; not quite enough to open 1◇.
With (b), 12 HCP, enough to open 1◇.

19. With any 5-3-3-2 distribution, open with 12+ HCP; pass with less.

20. With any 5-4-2-2 distribution, open with 12+ HCP, pass with less. However, if all 11 HCP are in the two long suits, and the five-card suit is strong, open.

a) ♠A Q 8 7 6 ♡K 4 ◇Q 8 7 5 ♣4 2
b) ♠A Q 10 5 4 ♡3 2 ◇K Q 5 4 ♣3 2

With (a), pass. With (b), open 1♠. All 11 points are in the two long suits. Concentrated strength in long suits is a plus.

21. With any 5-4-3-1 distribution, open with 12+ HCP; pass with 10 HCP or less. With exactly 11 HCP, open if the five-card suit is strong. If the five-card suit is weak, consider the rebid problem if partner responds in your short suit. If it will be awkward, pass; if it won't, open.

   a)   ♠A 4 3 ♡K Q 10 8 7 ♢2 ♣Q 7 6 5
   b)   ♠A 4 3 ♡K 9 7 6 5 ♢A 10 7 6 ♣2
   c)   ♠A 4 3 ♡K 9 7 6 5 ♢2 ♣A 10 7 6

With (a), open 1♡; your five-card suit is strong and can be rebid after a 2♢ response.

With (b), open 1♡; you have an easy 2♢ rebid if partner responds 2♣; raise 1♠ to 2♠.

With (c), pass; you have an awkward rebid if partner responds 2♢. The idea is to avoid rebidding weak five-card suits, if possible. If you do open, the least of evils is repeating your hearts. Anything else is out of sight.

22. With any 5-5 distribution, open with 11+ HCP, pass with less.

   a)   ♠A Q 6 5 4 ♡K J 5 4 3 ♢5 4 ♣3
   b)   ♠A 9 8 7 2 ♡3 ♢A K 9 5 4 ♣5 2

With (a), pass, not quite enough to open. With (b), an easy 1♠ opening bid.

23. With a six-card suit, open with 11+ HCP, pass with less. However, with 6-4 distribution, open with 10 HCP if the six-card suit is strong (three of the top five honors).

   a)   ♠4 ♡K Q 8 7 6 5 ♢A 7 6 ♣Q 5 4
   b)   ♠4 ♡A 9 7 6 5 4 ♢K J 7 5 ♣Q 2
   c)   ♠4 ♡A Q 10 5 4 3 ♢K J 7 5 ♣3 2

With (a), open 1♡; you have 11 HCP.

With (b), pass; with 10 HCP and 6-4 distribution, you need a stronger six-card suit.

With (c), open 1♡; your hearts are strong enough.

24. With 5-6 distribution in adjacent suits, the five-card suit being the higher-ranking, open the six-card suit with 14+ HCP; with 10-13 HCP open the five-card suit. With less, pass.

a) ♠3 ♡AQJ76 ◇A108743 ♣2
b) ♠3 ♡AQJ76 ◇AQJ876 ♣2
c) ♠3 ♡KQ876 ◇A98765 ♣2

With (a), open 1♡. With (b), open 1◇. With (c), pass.

25. Add 1 point to any hand that has three tens each connected with a higher honor, or two 10-9 combinations that are attached to four-card suits or longer.

a) ♠AJ10 ♡AJ104 ◇Q104 ♣876
b) ♠A10932 ♡A1094 ◇A32 ♣3

Both of these hands are worth at least 1 extra point.

26. Unless you fear the heavens will part, open 1♡ or 1♠ in third or fourth seat with a strong four-card suit and a minimum hand.

♠54 ♡AKJ10 ◇10987 ♣A104

In third or fourth seat, open 1♡. If you play four-card majors, open 1♡ in any seat. This hand is also worth a 1♡ overcall if the opening bid to the right is 1♣ or 1◇.

27. If you feel the decision is close about whether or not to open, let the intermediate cards in the long suits be the deciding factor. (See Tips 21, 22 and 23.)

*28. With a broken six-card minor and 15 HCP, open 1NT if you have stoppers in the other three suits.

♠K4 ♡K9 ◇KQ8 ♣A97654

Live a little, open 1NT. More descriptive than opening 1♣ and rebidding 2♣ after a one-level response.

THE FIRST RESPONSE

°29. Assume partner opens 1♣ and you have five diamonds along with a four-card major. With less than 11 HCP, respond in the major. With 11 or more HCP, respond in diamonds and bid the major next. With 11+ HCP you are strong enough to make two bids so bid the longer suit first. However, if the diamonds are very strong and the spades very weak, respond 1◊.

West	North	East	South
	1♣	pass	?

a) ♠ A 8 7 5 ♡ 7 6 ◊ K J 7 6 2 ♣ 6 5
b) ♠ A 8 7 5 ♡ 7 6 ◊ A K J 9 2 ♣ 6 5
c) ♠ 10 7 4 3 ♡ 9 3 2 ◊ A K J 10 8 ♣ 9

With (a), respond 1♠. You have less than 11 HCP.

With (b), respond 1◊. You are strong enough to bid both suits if necessary. With (c), break the rule and respond 1◊.

°30. Do not respond in a suit that has only four small cards when you have an opening bid or better. There may be a slam and you could wind up in the wrong suit.

West	North	East	South
	1♣	pass	?

♠ A K Q 10 ♡ 9 4 3 2 ◊ A J 4 ♣ J 8

Respond 1♠. Trust me on this one even though it is an exception.

31. With 4-4 in the majors, respond 1♡ to a minor-suit opening bid. With 5-5, respond in the higher-ranking suit first.

West	North	East	South
	1♣	pass	?

a)   ♠ A J 9 8   ♡ Q 9 6 5   ◇ 5 4   ♣ J 9 8

b)   ♠ Q 7 6 5 4   ♡ A K J 10 5   ◇ 5 4   ♣ 3

With (a), respond 1♡. With (b), respond 1♠.

32.   With a five-card major and 5 HCP or a six-card major with 4 HCP, do not pass a minor-suit opening bid if second hand passes.

West	North	East	South
	1♣	pass	?

a)   ♠ K Q 9 7 6   ♡ 9 8 7   ◇ 5 4 3   ♣ 3 2

b)   ♠ K J 9 7 6 5   ♡ 4 3   ◇ 5 4   ♣ 8 7 5

Respond 1♠ with both hands — in an audible voice! If you play weak jump responses, bid 2♠ with (b).

*33.   With four diamonds and four hearts, respond 1♡ to a 1♣ opening bid. However, if you have four small hearts and four gigantic diamonds, respond 1◇. See Tip 29.

West	North	East	South
	1♣	pass	?

a)   ♠ 3 2   ♡ K 8 4 2   ◇ A Q 7 6   ♣ J 3 2

b)   ♠ 3 2   ♡ 7 6 4 2   ◇ A K J 10   ♣ J 3 2

With (a), respond 1♡. With (b), respond 1◇. Partner may wind up on lead!

34.   With game-going responding hands, respond in your longer suit first. Reread this one.

35.   It is mega-important to know what bidding methods your opponents are using as well as their defensive agreements in regard to signaling and leads.

36. An important agreement to make with partner is whether a two-level response followed by a rebid in that suit at the three-level is forcing or invitational showing 8-10 HCP with a powerful six- or perhaps seven-card suit (AKJ10xxx). Some play that any two-level response is a game force, others do not.

West	North	East	South
	1♡	pass	?

a) ♠753 ♡64 ◇AKQ1074 ♣32
b) ♠J53 ♡64 ◇K87654 ♣KQ

With (a), respond 2◇ and rebid 3◇, not forcing, but invitational to 3NT. If you play that a 3◇ rebid would be game-forcing, start with 1NT.

With (b), respond 1NT. This 9-point hand does not compare with (a), a hand that has a likely six tricks,.

*37. With 4-3-3-3 distribution and 6-7 HCP plus three-card support for partner's major-suit opening, respond 1NT. With the same distribution and 8-10 HCP, raise partner to the two-level. However, if your cards in partner's major are headed by the AK, AQ, or KQ, raise regardless.

West	North	East	South
	1♠	pass	?

a) ♠J54 ♡Q876 ◇Q87 ♣Q98
b) ♠AQ10 ♡8765 ◇543 ♣1087
c) ♠1075 ♡KQ4 ◇A876 ♣432

With (a), respond 1NT to slow down the auction with this piece of cheese.
With (b), raise to 2♠. All of your strength is in partner's suit.
With (c), raise to 2♠, more encouraging than 1NT.

38. A direct natural response of either 2NT or 3NT denies a singleton. A 1NT response may contain a singleton — or even a void!

West	North	East	South
	1♠	pass	?

a) ♠3 ♡A Q 8 7 ◇K Q 4 2 ♣K 10 8 7
b) ♠— ♡K 8 7 6 ◇Q 10 8 7 6 ♣Q 5 4 3

With (a), respond 2♣. Do not even think of responding 2NT. You can bid notrump later if you wish.

With (b), respond 1NT.

39.   A 2♡ response to a 1♠ opening bid promises at least five hearts. A 2♣ or 2◇ response to a major-suit opening bid can be made on a four-card suit but is usually longer.

40.   In competition, a response of either 2♡ or 2♠ promises at least a five-card suit. With a four-card major, think 'negative double.'

West	North	East	South
	1◇	1♠	?

a) ♠3 2 ♡A J 10 4 3 ◇4 2 ♣K Q J 4
b) ♠3 2 ♡K Q 7 4 ◇4 3 2 ♣A K 9 8

With (a), bid 2♡. You have your five-card suit, and you have your 10+ HCP.

With (b), double. Check out the chapter on Negative Doubles.

OPENER'S REBID

41. After a two-level response, a new suit by the opener is forcing.

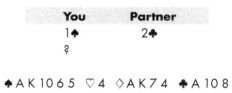

You	Partner
1♠	2♣
?	

♠ A K 10 6 5   ♡ 4   ◇ A K 7 4   ♣ A 10 8

Rebid 2◇. Do not crowd the auction with a jump shift, you've got too much describing to do.

42. After a single raise, a new suit is forcing.

You	Partner
1♣	2♣¹
?	

1. Weak.

You hold:

♠ 8 7   ♡ A Q 5   ◇ A 4   ♣ A K 9 8 7 4

Bid 2♡, forcing, If partner rebids 3♣, bid 3◇, forcing. What you are hoping is that partner with a spade stopper will bid 3NT. Bidding on after a single raise shows 16+ HCP. It does *not* mean that you are running away from a short club opening.

*43. Avoid rebidding weak five-card suits. Look for something else. This is a recording.

You	Partner
1♣	1◇/1♡/1♠
?	

♠KJ10 ♡AK3 ◇32 ♣K8765

If partner responds 1◇, rebid 1NT. If partner responds 1♡ or 1♠, raise to the two-level. If your religion forbids three-card raises, rebid 1NT and at least consider attending a different church[1].

You	Partner
1◇	1♠
?	

a) ♠AK4 ♡54 ◇AJ105 ♣J987
b) ♠Q43 ♡AQ ◇AJ105 ♣10987

With either hand, bid 1NT over a 1♡ response.
   With (a), raise 1♠ to 2♠. With (b), rebid 1NT.

44. You can often treat a five-card suit headed by four or five of the top five honors as if it were a six-card suit.

♠32 ♡876 ◇A54 ♣AKQJ9

Open 1♣ and rebid 2♣ over any one-level response.

45. With a minimum hand and 2=2=5=4 distribution, open 1◇ and rebid 2♣ over a major-suit response. However, if the major-suit doubletons are strong, rebid 1NT.

---

1. For non-churchgoers: With 4-4 in the minors, 3-2 in the majors, and a hand not strong enough to open 1NT, open the stronger minor. If partner responds in the doubleton suit, rebid 1NT; if partner responds in the three-card major suit, raise if the doubleton is small, rebid 1NT if the doubleton has the queen, king, or ace.

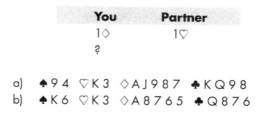

You	Partner
1◇	1♡
?	

a) ♠94 ♡K3 ◇AJ987 ♣KQ98
b) ♠K6 ♡K3 ◇A8765 ♣Q876

With (a), rebid 2♣. With (b), rebid 1NT.

*46. With 3=1=5=4 or 1=3=5=4 distribution, open 1◇. If partner responds in the singleton suit, rebid 2♣, not 1NT.

You	Partner
1◇	1♡/1♠
?	

♠8 ♡A43 ◇J10765 ♣AK54

After a 1♡ response, raise to 2♡. If you play that a raise promises four-card support, rebid 2♣. Avoid rebidding 1NT with a small singleton in partner's suit. Partner, holding a six-card suit, will play you for at least a doubleton and usually bid too much.

47. With 3=1=5=4 or 1=3=5=4 distribution, open 1◇. If partner responds in your three-card major, raise with 11-14 HCP. With 15-17 HCP, rebid 2♣ and then support the major.

You	Partner
1◇	1♡
?	

a) ♠3 ♡A76 ◇KQ765 ♣QJ98
b) ♠3 ♡AK6 ◇KQ765 ♣QJ98

With (a), raise to 2♡.
  With (b), bid 2♣ and then support hearts if partner bids again.

*48. With 4=3=2=4 or 4=3=4=2 distribution and 12-14 HCP, open one of the minor. If partner responds 1♡, rebid 1♠. However, if the hearts are strong and the spades weak, raise to 2♡.

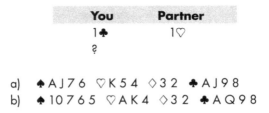

You	Partner
1♣	1♡
?	

a) ♠ A J 7 6 ♡ K 5 4 ◇ 3 2 ♣ A J 9 8
b) ♠ 1 0 7 6 5 ♡ A K 4 ◇ 3 2 ♣ A Q 9 8

With (a), rebid 1♠. With (b), rebid 2♡. Some players always rebid 1♠, but limiting your hand with a single raise will seldom get you in trouble. Rebidding 1♠ and later supporting hearts shows extra values, distributional or otherwise, in some sequences. (See next tip.)

49. Indirect support is stronger than direct support. Indirect support at the two-level is invitational; at the three-level, forcing. Both show three-card support.

You	Partner
1♣	1♡
1♠	

♠ A K 8 7 ♡ A J 4 ◇ 4 ♣ K 1 0 5 4 3

If partner's rebid is 1NT, bid 2♡, invitational, 14-16 HCP along with a singleton diamond.
   If partner's rebid is 2NT, bid 3♡, forcing.

50. After you open 1♡ or 1♠, partner responds 1NT, and you bid a lower-ranking suit at the two-level, a return to your major at the two-level shows a doubleton, not three-card support. With three-card support, the suit is normally raised immediately.

You	Partner
1♡	1NT
2♣	2♡

Partner figures to have two hearts, not three. If he has three hearts, he has a malnourished hand. See Tip 37.

51. A jump shift followed by a simple return to partner's original suit shows three-card support, not four.

You	Partner
1◇	1♠
3♣	3◇
3♠	

♠ A Q J   ♡ 2   ◇ A J 8 4 2   ♣ A K 9 4

Your bidding shows three-card spade support. With four spades, jump in spades directly or make a splinter jump, more about that later.

52. Anytime you skip over three bids, including notrump, to rebid your original suit, you show a six-card suit (exceptionally a five-card suit headed by four of the top five honors).

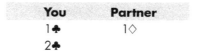

You	Partner
1♣	1◇
2♣	

You have shown six clubs because you have skipped over 1♡, 1♠ and 1NT to rebid your suit.

53. Rebidding a suit three times tends to show a seven-card suit or at the very least a strong six-carder.

You	Partner
1♡	1♠
2♡	2NT
?	

♠ 4   ♡ A J 9 7 5 4 2   ◇ K 7 5   ♣ Q 4

Rebid 3♡, not forcing, showing a seven-card suit with a minimum opening bid.

°54. With a six-card minor and three-card support for partner's major, rebid the minor if the suit is strong. If the suit is weak and the support is strong, raise the major. With marginal hands, rebid the minor if you are the stronger declarer, raise the major if partner is. (Don't tell partner why you are always rebidding your suit!)

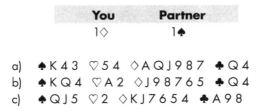

You	Partner
1◇	1♠

a) ♠K43 ♡54 ◇AQJ987 ♣Q4
b) ♠KQ4 ♡A2 ◇J98765 ♣Q4
c) ♠QJ5 ♡2 ◇KJ7654 ♣A98

With (a), rebid 2◇. With (b), raise to 2♠. With (c), raise to 2♠ with a good partner, rebid 2◇ with your regular one.

55. With a six-card minor, 16-17 HCP, 6-3-2-2 distribution and stoppers in the unbid suits, rebid 2NT over a one-level response rather than jump to the three-level in your six-card suit.

You	Partner
1◇	1♠
?	

♠54 ♡AQ ◇AKJ1043 ♣K43

Rebid 2NT rather than 3◇. If partner had responded 1♡, you would rebid 3◇ since you have no spade stopper.

56. With three four-card suits and a singleton diamond, open 1♣ and rebid 1♡ over a 1◇ response; if you rebid 1♠, you deny four hearts.

You	Partner
1♣	1◇
?	

♠AJ98 ♡J1076 ◇2 ♣AK76

Rebid 1♡. If partner has four spades, you will hear about it... right now.

57. With 5=4=4=0 distribution, open 1♠. If partner responds 2♣, your void suit, rebid 2♡, not 2◇. If you rebid 2◇, you deny four hearts.

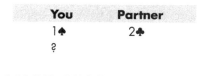

You	Partner
1♠	2♣
?	

♠ A J 9 8 7   ♡ K 8 7 6   ◇ A Q 7 6   ♣ —

Rebid 2♡.

58. With a six-card major and a four-card minor, rebid the major with 11-13 HCP; rebid the minor with 14-16 HCP.

You	Partner
1♡	1♠
?	

a) ♠ 2   ♡ A Q 10 5 4 3   ◇ K 4   ♣ Q J 7 6

b) ♠ 2   ♡ A Q 8 7 6 5   ◇ K 4   ♣ A Q 7 6

With (a), rebid 2♡ and, if you get another chance, bid 3♣ next to show a minimum 6-4. With (b), rebid 2♣ and then rebid the hearts to show a forward-going 6-4.

59. With an independent six-card major (one that can play opposite a singleton without shedding any tears) along with a four-card minor, either rebid the major or jump in the major after a one-level response. No need to offer partner an alternative trump suit. You know which suit you want to be trumps. This tip assumes you are not strong enough to make a jump shift.

You	Partner
1♡	1NT
?	

a) ♠ 2   ♡ K Q J 10 5 4   ◇ K 4   ♣ Q 10 7 6

b) ♠ 2   ♡ K Q J 10 5 4   ◇ K 4   ♣ A J 9 4

With (a), rebid 2♡. With (b), rebid 3♡.

60. With 5-5 distribution and a forward-going hand, open the higher-ranking suit and rebid the lower-ranking suit twice — even after partner gives you preference to your first suit.

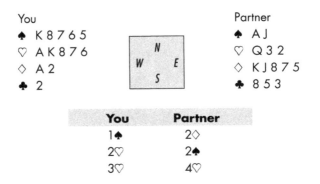

You	Partner
♠ K 8 7 6 5	♠ A J
♡ A K 8 7 6	♡ Q 3 2
◇ A 2	◇ K J 8 7 5
♣ 2	♣ 8 5 3

You	Partner
1♠	2◇
2♡	2♠
3♡	4♡

Responder is allowed to prefer spades with a strong doubleton rather than rebid 2NT without a club stopper or raise hearts with only three-card support (four-card support for a second suit is promised in blood). Catering to this possibility, your 3♡ rebid shows partner that fifth heart. Sure enough, a connection is made. Partner has two spades and three hearts. What did you expect? I made up the hand.

61. In a similar vein, with 5-4-2-2 distribution, do not necessarily insist upon your five-card suit even after a preference.

Partner	You
	1♠
1NT	2♡
2♠	?

♠ Q J 7 6 5   ♡ A 10 8 2   ◇ A K   ♣ K 4

Bid 2NT. Do not continue in spades! Partner almost for sure has a doubleton spade (would have raised spades with three). Rebid 2NT to show a forward-going balanced hand with 16-17 HCP. Partner knows you have five spades.

62. Now that you are getting into this, consider this distribution: 5-3-4-1. If you are strong enough, open the five-card suit, rebid the four-card suit and in some cases show the three-card suit as well. What fun!

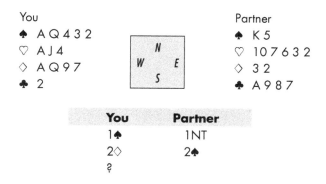

You	Partner
♠ A Q 4 3 2	♠ K 5
♡ A J 4	♡ 1 0 7 6 3 2
◇ A Q 9 7	◇ 3 2
♣ 2	♣ A 9 8 7

You	Partner
1♠	1NT
2◇	2♠
?	

Rebid 3♡, completing the picture of your hand. You cannot have four hearts in this sequence, you would have rebid 2♡. If you rebid 3♡, partner will raise to 4♡, and you are in the right contract. (See Tip 57.)

*63. With 4-3-3-3 distribution (the four-card suit a major) and 12-14 HCP, open 1♣ and rebid 1NT over a response in your three-card suit. Do not rebid the major suit. This tip will be considered heresy by some!

You	Partner
1♣	1♡
?	

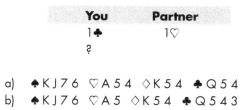

a) ♠ K J 7 6 ♡ A 5 4 ◇ K 5 4 ♣ Q 5 4
b) ♠ K J 7 6 ♡ A 5 ◇ K 5 4 ♣ Q 5 4 3

With (a), rebid 1NT, not 1♠. This tip assumes partner has a checkback method to determine whether you have bypassed a four-card major. With no checkback method, rebid 1♠.

With (b), rebid 1♠. Playing a checkback method, when you rebid a major after opening 1♣, you guarantee at least four clubs.

64. Bidding twice opposite a silent partner shows extra values, 15-17 HCP minimum. Bidding three times opposite a silent partner shows a hand in the 18-20 HCP range. Bidding four times opposite a silent partner hints strongly of a death wish!

RESPONDER'S REBID

65. A new suit by the responder is unlimited and forcing unless opener rebids 1NT.

66. If a one-level responder wishes to sign off or make weak noises (6-9 HCP), the weak rebids are: pass, repeating the original suit, returning to opener's first suit at the cheapest level or bidding 1NT.

Partner	You
1◇	1♡
1♠	?

a) ♠87 ♡KQ9743 ◇J4 ♣J54
b) ♠87 ♡KJ842 ◇32 ♣QJ97
c) ♠3 ♡A7654 ◇Q54 ♣8743
d) ♠Q54 ♡KJ432 ◇2 ♣5432

With (a), rebid 2♡, showing a six-card suit or a *very* strong five-carder, typically ♡AQJ10x.

With (b), rebid 1NT. Do not even think of rebidding those seedy hearts!

With (c), return to 2◇. Partner must have diamond length. Check Tip 5. With (d), pass.

67. One-level responding hands in the 10+ to 12 HCP range are expected to make invitational second bids after opener shows a minimum. These invitational second bids are 2NT or bidding at the three-level any suit that has already been bid.

Opener	Responder
1◇	1♡
1♠	2NT[1]

1. 11-12 HCP, not forcing.

Opener	Responder
1◇	1♡
1♠	3♡[1]

1. 9-11 HCP, six-card suit, not forcing.

Opener	Responder
1◇	1♡
1♠	3◇[1]

1. 11-13 support points, not forcing.

Opener	Responder
1◇	1♡
1♠	3♠[1]

1. 11-12 support points, not forcing.

68. After a one-level response, holding game-going values, rebid game if an eight-card major-suit fit has been uncovered. Bid game with an independent major suit or rebid 3NT, with a suitable hand.

Partner	You
1◇	1♡
1♠	?

a)   ♠76 ♡AKJ9843 ◇K4 ♣43
b)   ♠A987 ♡AKJ87 ◇K10 ♣97
c)   ♠654 ♡AK104 ◇83 ♣AQJ4

With (a), bid 4♡; 3♡ is not forcing.
   With (b), bid 4♠; 3♠ is not forcing.
   With (c), bid 3NT; 2NT is not forcing.

69. When as a one-level responder you want to be in game but don't know which game, bid a new suit to continue the force. If this new suit happens to be the fourth suit, the bid may be artificial.

Partner	You
1♢	1♡
1♠	?

a) ♠A4 ♡AKJ43 ♢J1054 ♣76
b) ♠K72 ♡AK765 ♢K2 ♣432

With (a), bid 2♣. You are not sure whether this hand belongs in hearts, diamonds or even notrump. Bid 2♣ to find out more about partner's hand. Partner is not supposed to bid notrump without a stopper in the fourth suit. A three-level jump to 3♢ or 3♡ would not be forcing.

With (b), bid 2♣. Once again, you cannot be sure whether this hand belongs in a suit or in notrump. Bid 2♣ to find out more about partner's hand.

•70. After the fourth suit, any subsequent rebid by the responder at the three-level is game forcing.

Opener	Responder
1♢	1♡
1♠	2♣
2NT	3♣/♢/♡/♠[1]

1. All forcing rebids

•71. The fourth suit is a way for the responder to make a forcing bid to ask for more information. The question is: Is it always a game force?

Opener	Responder
1♢	1♡
1♠	2♣*
2♢	2♡/2♠/2NT

Forcing or not? Read on...

Some play that fourth suit is a game force. Period. Others play it as a game force after a two-level response and forcing to at least 2NT after a one-level response.

•72. After opener makes a jump rebid, a three-level rebid in responder's original suit is forcing.

Opener	Responder
1◇	1♡
2NT/3◇	3♡¹

1. Forcing.

Those who play Wolff Signoff (See Tip 494) use 3♣ after 2NT to start a non-forcing sequence that can end in 3♡.

⁕73. When a three-level rebid in responder's original suit is forcing, a jump to game instead shows a powerful six- or seven-card suit but little else.

Partner	You
1◇	1♡
2NT	?

a) ♠ 7 4 ♡ A Q 8 7 5 4 ◇ 9 3 ♣ Q 9 2
b) ♠ 7 4 ♡ A K J 10 9 3 ◇ 2 ♣ J 8 7 6

With (a), rebid 3♡, forcing, typically a six-card suit.

With (b), jump to 4♡ to emphasize the quality of the suit, but promise little outside. Armed with that specific knowledge, partner may be able to bid a slam.

74. Raising a second suit promises four-card support.

Partner	You
1♡	1♠
2♣	3♣

If you don't have at least four clubs, you had better have some pretty good reasons for your bid. One possibility is, 'Sorry partner, I had one of my spades in with my clubs.'

⁕75. A direct response of 2NT not only shows 13-15 HCP but also denies a singleton. However, a 2NT rebid, which shows 11-12 HCP, may contain a singleton.

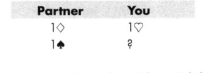

Partner	You
1◇	1♡
1♠	?

♠ K Q 4   ♡ K 10 5 4 3   ◇ 10   ♣ K 9 8 5

Rebid 2NT, not forcing.

Many play that a direct response of 2NT to a minor-suit opening shows 11-12 HCP, balanced, and is not forcing. Over a major, they use the direct jump to 2NT as Jacoby showing a game-forcing raise with primary trump support. Playing Jacoby, a direct response of 3NT shows 13-15 balanced. (See Tip 495.)

76.   Not playing Jacoby 2NT, a direct response of 3NT shows 16-17 HCP, balanced. A rebid of 3NT shows 13-15 HCP and may contain a singleton.

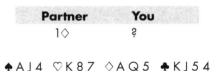

Partner	You
1◇	1♡
2◇	?

♠ A K Q   ♡ K Q 8 7 5   ◇ 4   ♣ J 10 5 4

Rebid 3NT.

*77.   Balanced hands in the 18-19 HCP range are too strong to respond 3NT directly. (See Tips 75 and 76.) One solution is to respond 2NT, forcing, and then over any minimum rebid partner makes, rebid 4NT, *invitational.* Talk this one over because you can't use this tip if you play the Jacoby 2NT response.

Partner	You
1◇	?

♠ A J 4   ♡ K 8 7   ◇ A Q 5   ♣ K J 5 4

Respond 2NT, and rebid 4NT. What happens now is on partner's head. You have shown your hand 'to a T'.

78. Responding in a lower-ranking suit and then bidding and rebidding a higher-ranking suit shows six cards in the lower-ranking suit and five cards in the higher-ranking suit.

Partner	You
1♣	?

♠ A J 8 7 6   ♡ A K 8 7 6 5   ◇ 2   ♣ 3

Plan to respond 1♡ and then to bid and rebid spades.

79. Do not rebid a new suit at the two-level with less than 11 HCP unless partner rebids 1NT.

Partner	You
1♣	1♡
1♠	?

♠ 5 4   ♡ A J 8 4 3   ◇ Q 10 8 7 6   ♣ 2

Try 1NT. Do not bid 2◇! You would be showing 11+ HCP.

80. After partner rebids 1NT, a new lower-ranking suit is not forcing.

Partner	You
1♣	1♡
1NT	?

♠ 5 4   ♡ A J 8 4 3   ◇ Q 10 8 7 6   ♣ 2

Rebid 2◇, not forcing. Contrast this to your rebid on the previous tip.

THE JUMP SHIFT BY THE RESPONDER

81. Think of a jump shift as a slam invitation, not a slam force.

82. Most jump shifts contain 15-18 HCP, not 19 or more. Strong six- and seven-card suits and/or support for partner's suit take up the point count slack.

83. If you are lucky enough to have 19 or more HCP and partner opens, it is up to you to push to slam unless:
    (i)   The hand is a misfit.
    (ii) Two cashing aces are missing.
    (iii) You have two quick losers in one suit.
    (iv) You are missing one ace plus the king of trumps.
    (v)   You have an eight-card trump fit and are missing one ace plus the trump queen.
    (vi) You have seen your partner play before.

84. A jump shift shows one of three types of hand:
    (i)   A one-suited hand — six or more cards in the suit.
    (ii) A hand with four or more cards in partner's suit.
    (iii) A balanced hand with a five-card suit and 16-18 HCP.

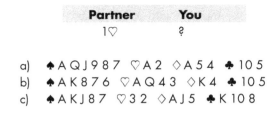

Partner	You
1♡	?

a) ♠ A Q J 9 8 7 ♡ A 2 ◇ A 5 4 ♣ 10 5
b) ♠ A K 8 7 6 ♡ A Q 4 3 ◇ K 4 ♣ 10 5
c) ♠ A K J 8 7 ♡ 3 2 ◇ A J 5 ♣ K 10 8

With (a), jump to 2♠, intending to rebid the suit.
    With (b), jump to 2♠, intending to return to hearts.
    With (c), jump to 2♠, intending to rebid notrump.

85.   Do not jump shift with a two- or three-suited hand (unless one of the suits is partner's) regardless of strength.

Partner	You
1◇	?

a) ♠ A K 7 6 ♡ A Q 7 6 ◇ 2 ♣ A Q 7 6
b) ♠ A K 8 7 ♡ A K 8 7 3 ◇ 2 ♣ A J 2

With both hands, respond 1♡. You do not have any of the three types of hand partner will be expecting for a jump shift. Discipline!

*86.   A jump shift in a major suit, followed by a second jump in the same major suit to game, is a specialized sequence. It shows a solid seven- or eight-card suit with one outside ace. Without the outside ace, bid the major at the one-level and then jump to game in the major next.

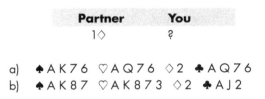

Partner	You
1◇	?

a) ♠ A K Q J 8 7 6 ♡ 4 ◇ 4 3 ♣ 10 6 5
b) ♠ 3 ♡ A K Q J 8 7 6 2 ◇ 4 3 ♣ A 6

With (a), respond 1♠ and then jump to 4♠.
    With (b) jump to 2♡ and then jump to 4♡.

87. After making a jump shift with primary support in partner's suit, return to partner's original suit if you have no side-suit singleton. With a side-suit singleton, bid the singleton suit instead. This is the Soloway convention and is quite popular.

Partner	You
1♡	2♠
2NT	?

a) ♠ A Q 8 7 6 ♡ A K 6 5 ◇ K 4 ♣ 8 7
b) ♠ A Q 8 7 6 ♡ A K 6 5 ◇ K 4 2 ♣ 2

With (a), rebid 3♡, denying a singleton. With (b), rebid 3♣, showing four hearts plus a singleton club. (Remember, you cannot have clubs. No jump shifts with two-suited hands!)

88. Another specialized jump shift is a jump followed by a jump return to partner's first suit. This rebid shows excellent trumps, a strong side suit, but denies a control in the other two suits.

Partner	You
1♡	?

♠ A Q J 7 6 ♡ A K Q 8 ◇ 5 4 ♣ 4 3

Jump to 2♠ and then jump in hearts.

*89. A jump shift can be made on a four-card suit providing responder has strong support for opener's first suit.

Partner	You
1♣	?

♠ K 4 ♡ 2 ◇ A K J 4 ♣ A 10 9 7 6 5

Jump to 2◇. This hand will be very difficult to describe if you begin with 1◇. A corollary to four-card jump shifts is that opener must avoid supporting directly without four-card support. Not too many are in love with this corollary. Some support directly with singleton or doubleton honors assuming partner always has a long, strong suit. But this may not be the case.

AFTER RESPONDER MAKES A STRONG JUMP SHIFT

90. As opener, regardless of your strength, it generally pays to make a minimum 'waiting' rebid waiting for partner to describe the jump shift.

You	Partner
1♣	2♠
?	

♠ A 4   ♡ 6 5   ◇ K J 4   ♣ A Q J 7 6 5

Although there is almost certainly a slam or grand slam, bide your time with a 3♣ rebid. Find out which type of jump shift partner has.

91. A jump rebid in your suit shows solidity; it does not show extra strength. In fact, it denies an outside ace.

You	Partner
1♡	2♠
?	

♠ 2   ♡ A K Q J 7 6   ◇ Q 10 4   ♣ 8 7 6

Jump to 4♡ to show a solid suit without an outside ace.

*92. Do not rebid any suit that does not have two of the top three honors! Partner does *not* have a second suit. Partner is interested in learning *where* your strength is located.

You	Partner
1♠	3♣
?	

♠ K 7 6 5 4   ♡ A K 10   ◇ Q 8 7 6   ♣ 2

Bid 3♡ rather than 3◇. Partner cannot have four hearts so there is no chance for a mix-up, he said smugly.

93. Before leaping to 4NT, Blackwood, it pays to set the trump suit with a forcing raise at the three-level when possible.

You	Partner
1◇	2♠
?	

♠ K J 4 2   ♡ 4   ◇ A K 7 6 3   ♣ K 5 4

Even though you are surely going to wind up in 6♠ or 7♠, set the suit with a raise to 3♠ before plunging into Blackwood. It helps when both partners know what the agreed suit is. Reread this.

WHEN YOU OVERCALL

94. The range of a one-level overcall is wide. It could have as few as 8 HCP or as many as 16 HCP. However, some 16-point hands are more suitable to a takeout double and some hands in the 8-10 HCP range that do not possess a strong five-card suit headed by three honor cards are more suitable to passing!

West	North	East	South
		1◇	?

a) ♠87 ♡AQJ42 ◇543 ♣Q105
b) ♠87 ♡A7654 ◇QJ3 ♣Q105

With (a), overcall 1♡ — strong suit
   With (b), pass — horrible suit.
   Notice both hands have 9 HCP, but (a) is a much stronger hand.

95. A two-level overcall, particularly vulnerable, suggests a strong six-card suit with near opening bid values (10+ HCP) at the very least. The hand should contain at least one ace or king outside of the main suit. If it does not, chances are you are looking at a weak jump overcall. Note: A five-card suit headed by four of the top five honors or the next thing to it (AQJ98) can be treated as a six-card suit when it comes to a two-level overcall.

Neither vul.

West	North	East	South
		1♣	?

a) ♠A4 ♡54 ◇AQJ854 ♣876
b) ♠8 ♡Q75 ◇AQJ854 ♣876

With (a), overcall 1◇; you have a strong suit with an outside ace making it too strong for a weak jump overcall when holding a strong suit.
   With (b), overcall 2◇; you have no outside ace or king.

96. The range of a one-level overcall with a 5-3-3-2 hand pattern is 8-16 HCP. With more, double, and then bid the five-card suit.

West	North	East	South
		1♣	?

  a) ♠ K Q J ♡ A K 8 7 6 ♢ Q 5 4 ♣ 8 7
  b) ♠ A Q 4 ♡ A K J 5 4 ♢ K 5 4 ♣ 8 7

With (a), overcall 1♡. With (b), double and then bid hearts.

*97. A one-level overcall by a non-passed hand can be made on a *four-card* suit if the suit is headed by the AKQ, AKJ10, AKJ9, AQJ10, AQJ9 or KQJ10 and the hand has opening bid values. In addition, the distribution must not qualify for a takeout double (the first option) perhaps because of having four cards in opener's suit or perhaps because of lack of support for one of the unbid suits. P.S. Make sure your voice doesn't crack!

West	North	East	South
		1♡	?

  a) ♠ A K J 4 ♡ 7 4 3 2 ♢ Q 8 6 ♣ 3 2
  b) ♠ A K J 9 ♡ 7 4 3 2 ♢ A 5 3 ♣ 3 2
  c) ♠ A 1 0 8 3 ♡ J 4 3 2 ♢ Q 2 ♣ K Q J
  d) ♠ A Q J 9 ♡ 3 2 ♢ 1 0 9 8 7 ♣ A J 3

With (a), pass. Neither your suit nor your hand is strong enough.

With (b), overcall 1♠, perfect.

With (c), pass. Your suit is not nearly strong enough, and the ♡J is not counted. You don't have support for one of the unbid suits, so cannot double. Other than that, it's perfect for a 1♠ overcall.

With (d), double. No need to overcall on a four-card suit when your hand is suitable for a takeout double.

98. The most effective overcalls are those that take up the most bidding space from the opponents.

West	North	East	South
		1♣	1◇ or 1♠

A 1◇ overcall does not make life difficult for West, who can respond at the one-level. However, after a 1♠ overcall West is deprived of a one-level response in a red suit.

*99. When your right-hand opponent opens the bidding in one of your two five-card suits and you have 10-14 HCP, bid your other five-card suit at the one-level if possible. If you must go to the two-level, pass and await developments — unless you have very strong intermediates in the suit you plan to bid.

You hold:

♠4   ♡A 10 9 8 4   ◇Q 3   ♣A 9 7 3 2

If your right-hand opponent opens 1♣, overcall 1♡. If your right-hand opponent opens 1♡, pass (your club spots are not good enough for 2♣).

100. With two five-card suits and less than 19 HCP, overcall in the higher-ranking suit. With more, double. This tip assumes you are not playing Michaels. (See Tips 448, 449 and 450.)

West	North	East	South
		1♡	?

a)   ♠A Q J 8 7   ♡5   ◇Q 10 8 7 6   ♣3 2
b)   ♠A Q J 8 7   ♡5   ◇A K J 8 7   ♣10 2
c)   ♠A Q J 8 7   ♡5   ◇A K 9 8 6   ♣A 2

With (a) and (b), overcall 1♠. With (c), double. Too strong a hand to risk the hand being passed out in 1♠.

101. Avoid takeout doubles with six-card major suits unless you have 16+ HCP. Avoid takeout doubles with six-card heart suits unless you have at least three-card spade support.

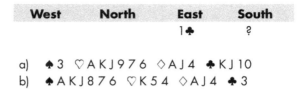

West	North	East	South
		1♣	?

a) ♠3 ♡AKJ976 ◇AJ4 ♣KJ10
b) ♠AKJ876 ♡K54 ◇AJ4 ♣3

With (a), overcall 1♡. Making a takeout double with a singleton spade (an unbid suit) is like crossing a busy intersection blindfolded... maybe worse.

With (b), double. When you double with a six-card spade suit, you can always correct to spades at the same level if partner gets rambunctious. Even so, when you double with a six-card major and then bid the suit, partner thinks you have five cards in the suit. If you double and then jump in your major you do show a six-card suit, so that's what you should do with the hand in example (b).

102. Vulnerable two-level overcalls promise strong suits plus opening bid or near opening bid values. Minor-suit two-level overcalls tend to show six-card suits, however an overcall of 2♡ is apt to be a five-carder.

103. Whereas a vulnerable two-level overcall generally shows three of the top five honors in the suit, a non-vulnerable two-level overcall need not be quite so strong. However, the strength of the hand should approximate an opening bid. Furthermore, one tends to bid more aggressively at matchpoints than at IMP scoring.

West	North	East	South
		1♡	?

a) ♠A2 ♡432 ◇KJ765 ♣A104
b) ♠A2 ♡43 ◇KQ1098 ♣A1042
c) ♠A2 ♡43 ◇KJ8762 ♣Q105
d) ♠A2 ♡43 ◇AJ10876 ♣Q105

With (a), pass at any vulnerability. You have a suit lacking intermediates, you have the worst distribution possible, 5-3-3-2, and you have three small cards in the suit bid to your right. These are all traps when considering an overcall.

With (b), overcall 2◇ at any vulnerability. Notice the difference in the diamond texture compared to (a). With (c), pass vulnerable, overcall 2◇ not vulnerable. With (d), overcall 2◇ at any vulnerability. The texture of the long suit is the deciding factor.

104. Overcalls in the fourth seat frequently depend upon the strength of your right-hand opponent's response. If your right-hand opponent has made a two-over-one response, beware! The opponents are in a power auction, and you should *only* bid with a strong suit to help direct the lead or suggest a sacrifice. Forget points. You are outgunned. The opponents figure to have at least 24 HCP between them, usually more.

West	North	East	South
1♠	pass	2♣	?

a) ♠ K J 4 ♡ A Q 8 7 6 ◇ A 9 8 ♣ J 4
b) ♠ 5 ♡ K Q J 9 8 4 ◇ Q 9 3 2 ♣ 3 2

With (a), pass with the speed of summer lightning. Your suit is seedy, you have losers from one end of your hand to another, and let's not forget you have the death distribution, 5-3-3-2. Worse, your partner figures to have 1 or 2 HCP. Do the math.

With (b), bid 2♡. After a two-over-one start, usually leading to a game contract, a fourth seat overcall should be thought of as a weak jump overcall, basically helping partner out on opening lead.

105. If your right-hand opponent makes a weak response, particularly a single raise, loosen up a bit. Two-level overcalls can be made with 9-11 HCP and a reasonable suit. Jump overcalls showing 13-15 HCP with a strong six-card suit are invitational, not weak. When the bid to your right is weak, a jump by you is strong.

West	North	East	South
1♡	pass	2♡	?

a) ♠ A K Q 8 7 ♡ 4 3 ◇ 1 0 9 7 6 ♣ 4 3
b) ♠ A K Q 8 7 4 ♡ 7 5 ◇ A Q 9 ♣ 1 0 6

With (a), make the bid that hits you in the face, 2♠. If opener passes, partner can place the opponents with 18-21 HCP and will know your strength to within a point or two. Not to worry.

With (b) leap to 3♠, invitational, showing about eight tricks.

106. In second seat, jump overcalls of 2NT are Unusual, showing 5-5 or 6-5 or 5-6 in the two lower-ranking unbid suits. The range is usually 7+ to 11 HCP.

(a)

West	North	East	South
		1♡/♠	?

♠ 4 ♡ 6 ◇ A 10 8 7 6 ♣ K J 8 7 6 5

Overcall 2NT, and leave the rest to partner.

(b)

West	North	East	South
		1♣	?

♠ 4 ♡ K J 8 7 6 ◇ A J 9 8 7 6 ♣ 4

Overcall 2NT, showing a red two-suiter (the two lower-ranking unbid suits).

*107. A direct bid in the responder's suit is natural, typically showing a strong six-card suit and 9-12 HCP. (Some play that it promises an opening bid.)

West	North	East	South
1♣	pass	1♡	?

♠ 4 ♡ A K 10 9 7 6 ◇ Q 4 3 2 ♣ 8 6

Bid 2♡. Don't wait around! With a stronger hand (◇AQ32), pass, and then bid hearts.

WHEN PARTNER OVERCALLS

108. A single raise of an overcall is equal to the single raise of an opening bid — 7-10 support points. Give those raises!

109. With three-card major-suit support and a hand too strong for a single raise, cuebid.

West	North	East	South
1♡	1♠	pass	?

a)   ♠A87 ♡54 ◇KQ87 ♣Q765
b)   ♠A87 ♡54 ◇AK76 ♣K1065

With both hands, bid 2♡. If partner signs off in 2♠, pass with (a) and raise to 3♠ with (b).

110. With four-card support and a hand too strong for a single raise, make a jump cuebid. The jump cuebid is invitational: think of it as a limit raise showing four-card support.

West	North	East	South
1♡	1♠	pass	?

♠KJ43 ♡87 ◇AQ98 ♣J43

Bid 3♡. If partner rebids 3♠, you can pass if you like.

111. Jump raises of overcalls are preemptive (thus the need for the cue-bids). Jump raises promise primary support, 3-6 HCP, and should contain a singleton or two doubletons, particularly when vulnerable.

West	North	East	South
1♡	1♠	2♡	?

♠A1043 ♡2 ◇J10543 ♣876

Bid 3♠. Do not make the sissy bid of 2♠. There is no way you are going to buy this hand in 2♠. You might as well tell partner what you have. This is an important tip.

112. With three-card major-suit support, it is rare to change suits. In theory, a change of suits denies three-card major-suit support.

West	North	East	South
1♣	1♠	pass	?

a)   ♠J 10 4 ♡7 6 ◇A K 9 8 6 ♣9 8 7
b)   ♠9 4 ♡4 2 ◇A K J 6 5 4 ♣9 4 3

With (a), bid 2♠. A 2◇ bid would deny three spades.
   With (b), bid 2◇, not forcing.

*113. In response to a one-level major-suit overcall, a change of suit is not forcing and a jump in a new suit is invitational.

West	North	East	South
1◇	1♡	pass	?

a)   ♠A K 8 7 6 ♡2 ◇5 4 3 ♣K 8 7 6
b)   ♠A K J 10 4 ♡2 ◇A 7 4 ♣Q 10 7 6

With (a), bid 1♠, not forcing and denying opening bid values.
   With (b), bid 2♠, invitational (13-15 HCP).

*114. In response to a *two-level* overcall, a change of suit is invitational; a jump in a new suit is forcing.

West	North	East	South
1♠	2♣	pass	?

a)   ♠8 2 ♡A Q J 9 4 ◇J 7 3 2 ♣K 3
b)   ♠8 2 ♡A K J 9 7 4 ◇A Q 5 ♣J 4

With (a), bid 2♡, invitational. With (b), bid 3♡, forcing.

*115. If partner's overcall is greeted with a negative double, make your normal raise with 7-10 HCP, cuebid with stronger raises, and redouble to show an opening bid lacking three-card support.

West	North	East	South
1◇	1♡	dbl*	?

  a)   ♠Q 8 7 ♡K 8 7 ◇4 3 ♣Q 10 7 6 5
  b)   ♠A Q 4 ♡K 8 7 ◇4 3 ♣Q 10 8 7 6
  c)   ♠A 10 8 7 ♡10 4 ◇4 3 2 ♣A K J 6

With (a), raise to 2♡. With (b), cuebid 2◇.

With (c), redouble. Note: Some play that the redouble simply shows the ace or king of partner's suit... period.

116. When partner overcalls in a minor suit and catches you with support, set your sights on 3NT. The cuebid is forward-going, asking for a stopper in the opponents' suit. The jump cuebid is used to show support with a singleton in the opponents' suit.

West	North	East	South
1♠	2♣	pass	?

  a)   ♠8 7 ♡A 8 7 3 ◇K 8 7 6 ♣J 4 3
  b)   ♠8 7 ♡A K 8 7 ◇K 8 7 6 ♣J 4 3
  c)   ♠K 8 7 ♡A Q 4 ◇10 6 5 2 ♣J 4 3
  d)   ♠4 ♡A 8 7 6 ◇K 8 7 6 ♣A J 5 4

With (a), raise to 3♣, the weakest raise, 7-9 support points.

With (b), cuebid 2♠ asking for a spade stopper with a forward-going hand. With (c), bid 2NT. Even with trump support, notrump takes priority with a stopper in the opponent's suit.

With (d), jump to 3♠ to show a strong hand in support of clubs with a singleton spade, 13-16 support points.

117. Know your ranges when it comes to bidding notrump in response to a one-level overcall. A 1NT response shows 8-12 HCP; a 2NT response shows 12+-14 HCP; 12-point hands are borderline, and a 3NT response shows 15-18 HCP. The 2NT response is not forcing.

West	North	East	South
1♣	1♠	pass	?

a) ♠75 ♡AQ4 ◇K1043 ♣J876

b) ♠92 ♡AQ4 ◇A954 ♣A1084

c) ♠J4 ♡AJ5 ◇KQJ9 ♣K1094

With (a), bid 1NT. With (b), bid 2NT. With (c), bid 3NT.

118. After partner overcalls and you respond in notrump, you promise one stopper, usually two, in the opponent's suit. You do not promise stoppers in each of the unbid suits, although it is a little easier on the nerves if you have them.

119. When considering a notrump response to a two-level minor-suit overcall, consider the degree of fit you have with partner's suit. If you have an honor in the suit, bid 2NT with 9-11 HCP, 3NT with more. If you don't have an honor, 10-12 is the range for a 2NT response.

West	North	East	South
1♠	2♣	pass	?

a) ♠AJ84 ♡J1043 ◇765 ♣K5

b) ♠AJ54 ♡J1043 ◇K543 ♣2

With (a), bid 2NT. The ♣K is a big, big card. With (b), pass. A singleton in partner's long suit should serve as a warning to bid conservatively. Another warning is your lack of intermediate spot cards. Your hand is not as strong as it counts out. It is more like a 7- or 8-point hand. Reread this.

120. Holding strong primary trump support, make a jump raise regardless of how weak you are on the outside. Do not make a single raise! Reread this one. Again.

West	North	East	South
1♡	1♠	pass/2♣/◇/♡	?

♠AQ1043 ♡32 ◇432 ♣432

Bid 3♠, preemptive, regardless of what East does.

THE OVERCALLER'S REBID

121. When partner changes suits, denying support for your suit, do not rebid your suit unless you have a strong six-card suit.

West	North	East	South
		1♡	1♠
pass	2♢	pass	?

a) ♠ A Q 7 6 5 ♡ 8 7 6 ♢ 4 ♣ A 1 0 8 6
b) ♠ A Q 1 0 9 7 6 ♡ 8 7 6 ♢ 4 ♣ A 1 0 8

With (a), pass. Partner doesn't have spades and you don't have diamonds. Get out while the getting is good. Partner's 2♢ bid is not forcing.

With (b), bid 2♠.

122. After you make a one-level overcall and partner bids 1NT or 2NT, a rebid by you in opener's suit is natural.

West	North	East	South
		1♣	1♡
pass	1NT	pass	?

♠ 5 ♡ K Q 8 7 6 ♢ 4 3 ♣ K Q J 7 6

Bid 2♣ to show a heart-club two-suiter.

123. After you overcall a minor-suit opening bid and partner passes, if you get another chance to bid, bidding the opener's minor suit is natural and not forcing. You hold:

West	North	East	South
		1♢	1♡
dbl*	pass	1♠	?

♠ 3 ♡ A K 9 8 4 ♢ K Q J 1 0 4 ♣ 3 2

Bid 2♢. The level is cheap and your suit is good enough.

124. A non-jump cuebid in response to a one-level overcall typically shows three-card support with 11-13 support points. In return, if your rebid goes beyond the two-level of your suit, you promise an opening bid. A rebid of your original suit shows a minimum. Bidding a lower-ranking suit, forcing, does not promise an opening bid but may contain one. A jump rebid to the three-level is invitational as is 2NT. A return cuebid is a game force.

West	North	East	South
		1◇	1♠
pass	2◇	pass	?

a) ♠AQ1054 ♡87 ◇K54 ♣876
b) ♠AQ10543 ♡87 ◇K4 ♣K98
c) ♠AJ876 ♡KQ54 ◇65 ♣65
d) ♠AJ876 ♡KQ54 ◇A3 ♣65
e) ♠AJ943 ♡K4 ◇AJ5 ♣987
f) ♠AJ943 ♡1087 ◇AJ4 ♣108
g) ♠A10876 ♡3 ◇87 ♣KJ876
h) ♠A10876 ♡3 ◇87 ♣AK876
i) ♠AK8742 ♡2 ◇AQ94 ♣K3

With (a), bid 2♠, showing 8-11 HCP.

With (b), bid 3♠, invitational, 12-13 HCP.

With (c), bid 2♡, forcing but not necessarily promising a good hand. Pass if partner bids 2♠.

With (d), bid 2♡, but continue on over 2♠.

With (e), bid 2NT, invitational, showing 12-14 HCP with diamond strength.

With (f), bid 2♠ — not strong enough to bid 2NT.

With (g), bid 2♠ — not strong enough to bid 3♣.

With (h), bid 3♣, forcing.

With (i), bid 3◇, a game force. There might be a slam.

THE TAKEOUT DOUBLE: WHEN TO AND WHEN NOT TO

125. The ideal distribution for a takeout double is 4-4-4-1 with a small singleton in the opener's suit. You can double with as few as 11 HCP if your right-hand opponent opens in your short suit.

126. With 4-4-4-1 distribution and 11-17 HCP, pass if they open one of your four-card suits. Later, if the opponents get together in your singleton suit, double for takeout.

West	North	East	South
		1◇	?

♠4 ♡AK76 ◇KJ76 ♣QJ87

Pass. If West responds 1♠ and East raises, double for takeout. If West responds 1NT and East passes, double to show a strong hand with short spades and likely strong diamonds.

127. Say you hold 4-4 in the majors and 3-2 in the minors. With 12-15 HCP, double if your right-hand opponent opens 1♣ or 1◇. Pass if your right-hand opponent opens 1♡ or 1♠.

With 16-18 HCP, plus stoppers in all suits, double if your right-hand opponent opens your short suit; otherwise, overcall 1NT. You can overcall 1NT with as few as 15 HCP if you have two stoppers in their suit.

West	North	East	South
		1♣/◇	?

a) ♠AK104 ♡AQ87 ◇543 ♣42
b) ♠AQ64   ♡QJ87 ◇AQ9 ♣K5
c) ♠AK98   ♡AQ98 ◇AQ10 ♣54

With (a), double 1♣ or 1◇. With (b), double 1♣; bid 1NT over 1◇. If you double 1◇ and partner bids 2♣, you need 19-20 HCP to rebid 2NT. With (c), double 1♣ or 1◇ — too strong to overcall 1NT over 1◇. (See Tip 131.)

128. Assume you hold some 4-4-3-2 distribution that does *not* include two four-card majors, and the opponents open in one of your four-card suits.

» With 14 or fewer HCP, pass. (See Tip 97.)

» With exactly 15 HCP, overcall 1NT if you have two stoppers in their suit; otherwise pass.

» With 16-18 plus a stopper in their suit, overcall 1NT. With 19+ HCP, double and then bid notrump if you don't connect in a major.

West	North	East	South
		1♡	?

a) ♠ 4 3 ♡ K J 9 8 ◇ A K 7 5 ♣ K 10 2
b) ♠ K 4 ♡ A Q 8 7 ◇ A J 7 6 ♣ J 10 4
c) ♠ K 4 ♡ Q 10 4 2 ◇ A J 10 ♣ A K Q J

With (a), pass — not strong enough to overcall 1NT, not to mention the spades!

With (b), overcall 1NT — 15+ HCP with two stoppers.

With (c), double intending to jump to 2NT if partner responds 1♠.

129. It is risky to make a takeout double with a small doubleton in an unbid major. In order to pull this one off, you should have 19+ HCP.

West	North	East	South
		1♣	?

a) ♠ 8 7 ♡ A Q 8 7 ◇ A K J 7 ♣ A J 7
b) ♠ 8 7 ♡ A Q 7 6 ◇ A J 8 7 ♣ A J 9

With (a), double. If partner bids 1♠, rebid 1NT, showing 18-19 HCP.

With (b), overcall 1NT directly. You are not strong enough to double and then bid 1NT over the expected spade response.

130. With 5-3 distribution in the majors and 4-1 in the minors, overcall your major suit at the one-level with 8-15 HCP, regardless of which suit is opened to your right. With a superior 15-count or more, double if they open your singleton suit; overcall if they do not.

West	North	East	South
		1◇	?

a) ♠A 9 2 ♡K Q 7 6 5 ◇4 ♣A J 4 3
b) ♠K 9 2 ♡A K 10 8 7 ◇4 ♣A J 10 3
c) ♠Q J 4 ♡K J 8 7 3 ◇4 ♣A K J 7
d) ♠A 9 3 ♡K Q 10 7 3 ◇4 ♣A K 8 7

With (a), bid 1♡ — not strong enough to double and then bid hearts.

With (b), double — a superior 15-count.

With (c), Bid 1♡ — an average 15-count.

With (d), double — strong enough to double and then bid hearts.

131. A takeout double followed by a 1NT rebid is stronger than overcalling 1NT directly.

West	North	East	South
		1♣	dbl
pass	1◇	pass	1NT

South has 18-19 HCP.

West	North	East	South
		1♣	1NT

South has 16-18 HCP. (Some 18-point hands are better than others.)

132. A takeout double followed by a suit rebid is stronger than overcalling the suit directly.

West	North	East	South
		1◇	dbl
pass	1♡	pass	1♠

South generally has either 17-18 HCP with 5-3-3-2 distribution or 16-18 HCP with 5-4-3-1 distribution.

West	North	East	South
		1◇	1♠

South has a range of 8-16 HCP! However with 8-10 HCP, you *must* have a strong suit.

133. After you make an overcall, you can still make a takeout double — providing the opponents find a fit and partner has not bid.

West	North	East	South
		1♡	1♠
2♡	pass	pass	?

♠ A K 8 7 6   ♡ 3 2   ◇ A J 4   ♣ K 6 5

Double — not quite strong enough to double and then bid spades (17+ HCP), but strong enough to bid spades and then double. This sequence shows 12 to a weak 16 HCP, shortness in the opponents' suit, and at least three cards in each of the unbid suits.

134. With eight or nine winners in your own hand plus a stopper in the opener's suit, overcall 3NT. Don't worry about points; this bid shows tricks!

West	North	East	South
		1♡	?

♠ K   ♡ K 4   ◇ A K Q 10 9 7 6   ♣ A 4 3

Are you a man or a mouse? Overcall 3NT. Stick a small club in with your spades if it will make you feel more secure.

135. With eight or nine winners in your own hand but no stopper in the major suit opened to your right, make a jump cuebid. (A new toy!) It asks partner to bid 3NT with a stopper in the opener's suit.

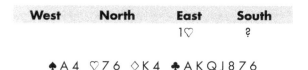

West	North	East	South
		1♡	?

♠A4 ♡76 ◇K4 ♣AKQJ876

Overcall 3♡. With a heart stopper, partner bids 3NT. If you do not hear 3NT, bid clubs.

136. A direct jump bid in the opponent's minor suit is natural, showing a seven-card suit with less than opening bid values.

West	North	East	South
		1♣	?

♠A4 ♡5 ◇876 ♣KQ109765

Bid 3♣ and let the opponents sort out what to do. They may not know that a double by the responder in this sequence is for takeout. Shh, don't tell them.

RESPONDING TO A TAKEOUT DOUBLE

137. When considering a suit response, do not count points for jacks and queens in the opener's suit. However, if you are planning to respond in notrump, count jacks and queens in the opponent's suit.

138. Add 1 point for an unbid five-card suit, 3 points for an unbid six-card suit, and 1 additional point for an unbid four-card suit (5-4 = 2 extra points, 6-4 = 4 extra points).

139. When responding in a suit, make a non-jump response with 0-8 revalued points, a jump response with 9-11 revalued points, and cuebid or bid game with 12+ revalued points.

West	North	East	South
1♡	dbl	pass	?

a) ♠AJ765 ♡543 ◇K4 ♣876
b) ♠AK65 ♡543 ◇K42 ♣876
c) ♠32 ♡543 ◇65 ♣AK10876
d) ♠AJ765 ♡Q54 ◇Q32 ♣54
e) ♠A87 ♡32 ◇AJ87 ♣KJ42

With (a), bid 2♠. Counting 1 extra point for your five-card suit, you have 9 points. This jump is not forcing.

With (b), bid 2♠. You have 10 points and are allowed to jump on a four-card suit.

With (c), bid 3♣. This hand is worth 10 points after adding 3 extra for your six-card suit.

With (d), bid 1♠. Do not count anything for the ♡Q. If the ♡Q were the ♣Q, bid 2♠.

With (e), bid 2♡ — too strong to make a jump response. The cuebid gives you time to sort things out.

140. With a four-card major and a five-card minor plus a hand too weak to jump, respond in the major.

West	North	East	South
1♡	dbl	pass	?

♠ K 10 4 3   ♡ 5 4   ◇ Q 7 6 5 4   ♣ 3 2

Respond 1♠.

*141. With a four-card major and a six-card minor, plus a hand too weak to jump, respond in the minor.

West	North	East	South
1♡	dbl	pass	?

♠ K 10 4 3   ♡ 4 3   ◇ Q 8 7 6 5 4   ♣ 5

Respond 2◇. You plan to bid spades later.

142. A 1NT response shows 7-10 HCP, a 2NT response 11-12 HCP, and a 3NT response 13-16 HCP. However, in response to a double of 1♡ or 1♠, a 1NT response can be shaded to 5-6 HCP. These responses promise at least one stopper in the opponent's suit, frequently two.

West	North	East	South
1♠	dbl	pass	?

a) ♠ K Q J 4   ♡ 8 7 6   ◇ 9 4 3   ♣ 7 6 5
b) ♠ Q 10 8 2   ♡ 6 5 3   ◇ 8 7   ♣ 8 7 6 5
c) ♠ A Q 4   ♡ K 5 4   ◇ J 10 7   ♣ K 10 6 5
d) ♠ A Q 3 2   ♡ K 4   ◇ Q 10 4 3   ♣ 4 3 2

With (a), bid 1NT.
   With (b), bid 2♣. You can only shade a 1NT response so much.
   With (c), bid 3NT.
   With (d), bid 2NT. You have 11 HCP — perfect.

143. You do not need stoppers in unbid suits to bid notrump, your partner has those. What you do need is at least one stopper, preferably two, in the opponents' suit.

144. When faced with a choice of cuebidding or jumping in notrump, strength in the opponent's suit is the deciding factor.

West	North	East	South
1♠	dbl	pass	?

a) ♠AQJ ♡10876 ◇KJ4 ♣J54
b) ♠A8 ♡A1097 ◇Q1043 ♣Q75

With (a), bid 2NT. With (b), start with 2♠.

145. A cuebid followed by a new suit is forcing.

West	North	East	South
1♡	dbl	pass	?

♠7 ♡A76 ◇Q98 ♣AQ10765

Bid 2♡ and then bid clubs to create a force. Do not make the lazy response of 3♣, a non-forcing response.

146. There is one case where you are allowed to cuebid with fewer than 12 points. When you have four cards in both unbid majors and 9+ HCP, you are allowed to cuebid. A cuebid followed by a raise is not forcing.

West	North	East	South
1◇	dbl	pass	?

a) ♠AJ54 ♡KJ98 ◇432 ♣54
b) ♠AJ54 ♡KJ98 ◇432 ♣K4

With (a), bid 2◇ and raise partner's likely major-suit response to the three-level, not forcing.

With (b), bid 2◇ and jump raise partner's likely major-suit response to game.

147. After you have made a minimum response to a takeout double show-ing 0-8, you are allowed to bid again opposite a silent partner. How-ever, to do so, you should have 6-8 points and either a five-card suit, a strong four-carder, or a second suit.

West	North	East	South
1♡	dbl	pass	1♠
2♡	pass	pass	?

♠ K Q 10 4   ♡ 7 6 5   ◇ J 10 3 2   ♣ 8 7

Bid 2♠. Partner must have spade support for the takeout double and you could have much less for your 1♠ response.

148. When your right-hand opponent bids, you are off the hook. Never-theless, make an effort to compete, if possible. A one-level squeak shows 5-8 points, a two-level squeak 6-9, and to come in at the three-level requires 8-10. With stronger hands, jump or cuebid.

West	North	East	South
1♡	dbl	2♡/3♡	?

♠ K J 9 8   ♡ 8 7 6   ◇ Q 10 7   ♣ 4 3 2

Over 2♡, bid 2♠. Over 3♡, pass.

149. If you must respond on a three-card suit, respond in the cheaper or cheapest three-card suit, not the strongest.

West	North	East	South
1◇	dbl	pass	?

♠ Q 9 8   ♡ 10 8 7   ◇ 8 7 6 5 4   ♣ J 2

You must bid something. Your diamonds are not nearly strong enough to con-sider a penalty pass. A 1NT response to a minor-suit takeout double shows 7-9 HCP with something in diamonds higher than an eight-spot! You have no alternative but to bid 1♡ — audibly, please.

*150. A *jump* cuebid shows a solid minor suit and asks partner to bid
notrump with a stopper in that suit.

West	North	East	South
1♡	dbl	pass	?

♠ 7 6 ♡ 8 7 ◇ 5 4 ♣ A K Q J 9 8 2

Bid 3♡. If partner has read this book, the meaning will be clear. If he hasn't,
why hasn't he?

151. Do not pass a low-level takeout double because of weakness. The only
excuse for passing is length and strength in the opponents' suit. You
should have either five cards headed by three of the top five honors
or six cards headed by two or three of the top five honors. With five
cards the intermediates must also be exceptional. If they are not, find
some bid, perhaps 1NT or 2NT.

West	North	East	South
1♡	dbl	pass	?

a) ♠ 4 ♡ A J 10 8 4 3 ◇ 4 3 ♣ J 8 7 6
b) ♠ 4 3 ♡ K Q J 9 8 ◇ 4 3 ♣ K 8 7 6
c) ♠ 4 3 ♡ K Q 6 5 4 ◇ 4 3 2 ♣ Q 7 6

With (a), pass. It doesn't get much better than this to make a penalty pass.
   With (b), pass — five hearts with good intermediates.
   With (c), bid 1NT — poor intermediates.

THE REBID BY THE TAKEOUT DOUBLER

152. Once you make a takeout double with minimum values, do not bid again unless partner makes a forcing bid or bids two suits requesting a preference.

West	North	East	South
		1◇	dbl
pass	2♡	pass	?

♠ A 10 5 4   ♡ K J 4   ◇ 5 4   ♣ A J 3 2

Pass. Partner's 2♡ is not forcing, and partner may have only four hearts.

153. A raise of a forced response shows 16-18 support points and guarantees primary support (four or more cards). In competition, the raise can be made with 15 support points but still guarantees primary support.

You hold:

♠ A K 8 7   ♡ K 9 4   ◇ 4 3   ♣ K J 7 6

a)

West	North	East	South
		1◇	dbl
pass	1♠	pass	?

b)

West	North	East	South
		1◇	dbl
pass	1♠	2◇	?

In auction (a), pass. In (b), compete to 2♠. If partner responds 1♡, pass in either case.

154. A jump raise shows 19-21 support points along with primary support.

West	North	East	South
		1♡	dbl
pass	1♠	pass	?

♠ A K 8 7   ♡ 2   ◇ A Q 8   ♣ K 10 9 8 5

Jump to 3♠, highly invitational.

155. After a forced response, a jump shift is invitational (18+ to 20 HCP). To force, cuebid and then bid a suit.

West	North	East	South
		1◇	dbl
pass	1♡	pass	?

a)   ♠ A Q 10 6 5   ♡ K Q 4   ◇ 4   ♣ A K J 8
b)   ♠ A Q 10 6 4   ♡ A K 4   ◇ 4   ♣ A K J 8

With (a), bid 2♠, highly invitational. With (b), cuebid 2◇, and then bid spades to create a force.

156. After a forced response, a new suit shows 16-18 HCP and is invitational.

West	North	East	South
		1◇	dbl
pass	1♠	pass	?

♠ A J 4   ♡ A K 8 7 6   ◇ 4   ♣ A 10 9 5

Bid 2♡, invitational. The 2♡ bid shows a five-card suit. Partner is expected to rebid a five-card spade suit looking at only one or two hearts.

157. After any jump response, including 2NT, a new suit is forcing.

West	North	East	South
		1◇	dbl
pass	2♡	pass	2♠

West	North	East	South
		1◇	dbl
pass	2NT	pass	3♡

In both cases, the last bid is forcing.

158. If partner responds at the two-level in competition, a new suit is invitational. If partner responds at the three-level in competition, a new suit is forcing.

a)

West	North	East	South
		1◇	dbl
2◇	2♡	pass	2♠

b)

West	North	East	South
		1◇	dbl
2◇	3♣	pass	3♠

In (a), 2♠ is invitational. In (b), 3♠ is forcing.

159. After a 1NT response, bidding a new suit (at least five cards) is not forcing, a jump is invitational. To force, cuebid, and then bid a suit.

West	North	East	South
		1♣	dbl
pass	1NT	pass	?

- a) ♠A 10 5 4 ♡K 8 7 6 ◇K J 10 5 4 ♣—
- b) ♠A J 7 2 ♡A 4 3 ◇K Q 10 4 3 2 ♣—
- c) ♠K Q 7 ♡A Q 9 7 4 2 ◇A 10 6 ♣A

With (a), bid 2◇, not forcing. With (b), bid 3◇, invitational. With (c), bid 2♣ and then bid hearts to create a force.

160. Doubling the same suit twice, or even three times, does not alter the original meaning of the double — takeout. However, if the second or third double comes at the game level, partner should only remove with an unbalanced hand.

West	North	East	South
		1♡	dbl
2♡	pass	pass	dbl
3♡	pass	pass	?

♠ A Q 8 7   ♡ 5   ◇ A Q 8 7   ♣ A K J 4

Double again. Even though you sound like a broken record, each successive double shows more and more strength. Your third double shows 18-20 HCP minimum.

OPENER'S REVERSE

161. Whenever opener bids two suits, forcing a *three*-level preference to the first suit, opener has **reversed**.

(a)	Opener	Responder	b)	Opener	Responder
	1♡	1♠		1◇	1♠
	2◇			2♡	

In (a), opener has not reversed. In (b), opener has reversed by forcing a three-level preference.

162. A reverse after a one-level response is a one-round force. A reverse after a two-level response is a game force.

163. Most reverses show five cards in the first suit and four in the second suit. A reverse can also be made with six cards in the first suit and four in the second; reverses with 4-4 distribution are rare.

164. After a one-level response, opener's reverse with 5-4 distribution shows 17+ HCP. With 6-4, the minimum to make a reverse is 15 HCP — providing the hand has concentrated strength in the two suits or the six-card suit has good intermediates. If neither condition exists, rebid the six-card suit.

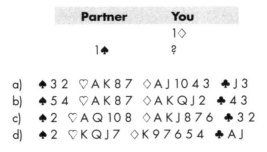

Partner	You
	1◇
1♠	?

a) ♠32 ♡AK87 ◇AJ1043 ♣J3
b) ♠54 ♡AK87 ◇AKQJ2 ♣43
c) ♠2 ♡AQ108 ◇AKJ876 ♣32
d) ♠2 ♡KQJ7 ◇K97654 ♣AJ

With (a), rebid 2◇. You are not strong enough to rebid 2♡ and force a three-level preference. A 1NT rebid hints at a common disease, 'notrumpitis.'

With (b), rebid 2♡. This hand is better than it looks because it has concentrated strength.

With (c), rebid 2♡. Concentrated strength in the two long suits is worth at *least* a 1 point upgrade.

With (d), rebid 2◇ — Neither the strength nor the intermediates in the long suit to reverse.

*165. After a *two*-level response, a reverse can be made with as few as 15 HCP and is a game force. Note: Some, who play that a two-level response is already a game force, play that after a two-level response, a reverse does not necessarily show extras.

Partner	You
	1◇
2♣	?

a) ♠42 ♡KQ87 ◇AKJ54 ♣43
b) ♠42 ♡KQ87 ◇AQ10 87 ♣A3

With (a), rebid 2◇.
   With (b), rebid 2♡.

166. Do not 'invent' a reverse with 5-5 distribution. Open the bidding in the higher-ranking suit.

♠3 ♡AKJ76 ◇AKJ87 ♣Q3

Open 1♡. To open this hand 1◇ is a colossal bridge blunder — actually, worse.

167. A jump reverse carries a special meaning and is discussed in the section on Splinter Jumps. See Tips 179 and 180.

168. In competition, a reverse may not always be a reverse. How's that again?

(a)

LHO	Partner	RHO	You
			1◇
2♣	2♡	pass	2♠

(b)

LHO	Partner	RHO	You
			1♡
2♣	2◇	pass	2♠

In (a), partner's two-level response outranked your first suit, making it impossible to rebid your original suit at the two-level had you wanted to. When that happens, mentioning a higher-ranking suit is not considered a reverse and can be done with a minimum opening bid. Ditto with a 2NT rebid.

In (b), partner's two-level response was in a lower-ranking suit than your suit. Had you wished, you could have rebid your original suit with a minimum. Therefore, in (b), you have reversed.

169. At times one has to create a reverse on a three-card suit with a 6-3-3-1 hand pattern in order to create a force.

Partner	You
	1♣
1♠	?

♠ A Q 4 ♡ K Q 4 ◇ 5 ♣ A K 8 7 6 5

Bid 2♡! Any jump in spades promises primary support; a jump in clubs is not forcing and you could lose a spade contract. A bid of 2♡, forcing, gives you a chance to support spades later to show three-card support. In addition, if partner raises hearts, showing four, partner must have five spades (with four hearts and four spades, partner responds 1♡).

WHEN PARTNER REVERSES

170. Do not pass. Life is too short; besides, the bid is forcing.

171. With 8+ HCP, insist upon game; with an opening bid, invite slam; with an opening bid and then some, bid slam if you find a fit.

*172. You must have some way to sign off after a reverse with hands in the 5-7 range.

> 1) Rebid your suit, forcing for one round but you can then pass partner's next bid if you wish.
> 2) Bid the fourth suit or 2NT, *whichever is cheaper*, asking partner to rebid his original suit (unless he has extras). After he does, pass or make a non-forcing preference in partner's second suit.

This is how you get out at the three-level in partner's first or second suit. Better reread this one.

Partner	You
1♣	1♠
2♦	?

a) ♠ K Q 8 7 4 ♡ 4 3 2 ♢ 8 7 6 ♣ J 4
b) ♠ K Q 8 7 ♡ 4 3 2 ♢ J 10 4 2 ♣ 7 6

With (a), rebid 2♠ and pass partner's next bid if it is not forcing. A new suit by partner would be forcing, but 2NT would not be forcing.

With (b), rebid 2♡, the fourth suit, cheaper than 2NT, and correct partner's forced 3♣ rebid to 3♢, not forcing. A direct raise to 3♢ is a game force. Also, when the fourth suit is used to start a signoff, 2NT is natural. When 2NT is used to start a signoff, the fourth suit shows a strong hand and should be considered natural.

*173. After a reverse, if you do not rebid your original suit, or the cheaper of the fourth suit or 2NT, the partnership is in a game-forcing auction.

174. With a notrump type hand, bid notrump. With 8-9 HCP, bid 2NT and then 3NT. With 10-12 HCP bid 3NT directly. With 13-14 HCP, bid 2NT and then 4NT, natural. Even if 2NT is used to start signoffs, it is still forcing. So if you follow it up with 3NT it negates the meaning of the signoff.

Partner	You
1♣	1♠
2◇	?

a) ♠K Q 8 7 ♡K J 10 ◇4 3 2 ♣6 5 4
b) ♠K Q 8 7 ♡K Q 9 ◇4 3 2 ♣7 6 5
c) ♠K 9 8 7 6 ♡K J 8 ◇K Q J ♣3 2

With (a), bid 2NT and then 3NT. In this case 2NT is natural since the fourth suit, 2♡, would be used to start a signoff.

With (b), bid 3NT.

With (c), bid 2NT and then 4NT.

175. A jump raise of partner's second suit shows good trumps. It is a mild slam try.

Partner	You
1◇	1♠
2♡	?

a) ♠A 8 7 6 5 ♡K Q 9 8 ◇4 3 ♣3 2
b) ♠A 8 7 6 5 ♡Q 5 4 3 ◇4 3 ♣K 2

With (a), bid 4♡ to emphasize your trump strength.

With (b), bid 3♡, a game force; your hearts are not strong enough to jump.

176. A return to partner's first suit is a forward-going bid. It is a game force. (See Tip 173.)

Partner	You
1◇	1♠
2♡	?

♠ A J 7 4 2   ♡ J 4   ◇ A 10 6   ♣ 8 7 6

Bid 3◇, a game force. If partner has three spades, you will hear 3♠ after your 3◇ bid.

SPLINTER JUMPS BY THE OPENER AND RESPONDER

177. A jump rebid by the opener one level higher than a jump shift is called a 'splinter jump'.

a)

Opener	Responder
1♡	1♠
2♣	

b)

Opener	Responder
1♡	1♠
3♣	

c)

Opener	Responder
1♡	1♠
4♣	

In (a), 2♣ is natural, normally showing five hearts and four clubs.

In (b), 3♣ is a jump shift, forcing to game. It neither promises nor denies spade support.

In (c), opener has made a splinter jump, a jump bid that is one level higher than a jump shift. A splinter jump promises primary support for responder's suit, a singleton in the jump suit and 18-20 support points. Opener might hold:

♠ K Q 7 6   ♡ A K 10 4 3   ◇ K J 5   ♣ 3

178. As the key to most successful slams is having the 'right' singleton, splinter jumps are invaluable.

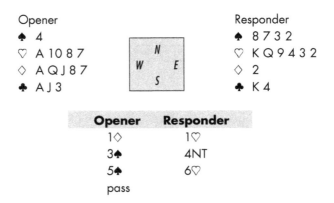

Opener	Responder
♠ 4	♠ 8 7 3 2
♡ A 10 8 7	♡ K Q 9 4 3 2
◇ A Q J 8 7	◇ 2
♣ A J 3	♣ K 4

Opener	Responder
1◇	1♡
3♠	4NT
5♠	6♡
pass	

The key bid in the sequence is opener's splinter jump to 3♠. Responder's hand has become enormous opposite spade shortness, and an easy slam is reached.

179. After a one-level response, a jump reverse is a splinter.

Partner	You
	1◇
1♠	?

a) ♠ 2 ♡ A K J 4 ◇ A Q J 8 7 ♣ K 3 2
b) ♠ A Q 7 4 ♡ 3 ◇ A K 7 5 4 ♣ K J 4

With (a), bid 2♡; a reverse is a one-round force.

With (b), bid 3♡, a jump reverse, a game force. The typical range is 16-18 HCP.

180. After a *two*-level response, a jump reverse is a splinter.

Partner	You
	1◇
2♣	?

♠ 4 ♡ A K 4 ◇ A J 8 7 6 ♣ K J 4 3

Bid 3♠, a jump reverse (splinter).

181. After a *two*-level response, a jump shift is a splinter.

Partner	You
	1♠
2◇	?

a) ♠A K J 8 7 ♡A K 10 5 4 ◇K J ♣3
b) ♠A K J 8 7 ♡2 ◇K J 8 7 ♣K 9 8

With (a), bid 2♡, forcing.

With (b), bid 3♡, a splinter. Many players use the jump shift to 3♡ as natural showing a strong 5-5 hand. Those players bid 3♡ with (a) and 3◇ or 4◇ with (b). This is something you and partner must discuss.

182. If you agree with the two previous tips, all second-round jumps by the opener after a two-level response are splinters because all new suit rebids are forcing.

183. If the opponents overcall, you can only splinter in their suit(s). In the long run, this tip will save you mucho grief. Experts, of course, make a few, very few, exceptions.

West	North	East	South
			1◇
1♡	?		

North can only splinter in hearts.

LHO	Partner	RHO	You
			1◇
1♡	1♠	2♣	?

a) ♠A Q 4 2 ♡3 ◇K Q 8 7 6 ♣A J 5
b) ♠A Q 4 2 ♡A J 5 ◇K Q 8 7 6 ♣3

With (a), jump to 3♡.

With (b), jump to 4♣.

°184. A jump one level higher than a splinter jump shows a void in the jump suit.

Partner	You
	1◇
1♠	?

a) ♠4 ♡AQ87 ◇KQ876 ♣AK4
b) ♠AQ87 ♡4 ◇KJ1054 ♣AK6
c) ♠KQ84 ♡— ◇AK8765 ♣K98

With (a), bid 2♡, forcing.

With (b), splinter to 3♡, a game force, showing a singleton heart.

With (c), splinter to 4♡, showing a heart void. Remember to add 5 points when holding a void with primary support for partner's suit. This hand logs in with 20 support points.

185. After partner has made an unlimited response, a splinter jump is a game force. After partner has made a limited response, a splinter jump is a slam try. See the following tip.

186. Opener can splinter after responder repeats a suit! These splinters are considered slam tries because responder is *limited*. After a suit has been rebid, a splinter jump shows three-card support.

Partner	You
	1◇
1♠	2♣
2♠	?

♠K76 ♡2 ◇AKQ104 ♣AJ87

Bid 4♡, a splinter jump showing three spades.

187. Splinter jumps are not toys. Unless both you and your partner are sure you can recognize one of these 'crazy' leaps, better to forget about them. There is no bridge disaster quite like a splinter disaster! However, they do make for great stories. A friend of mine once played a 1-1 fit! He said he was lucky because the trumps divided evenly — 6-5!

188. A first-round jump by the responder one level higher than a jump shift is a splinter.

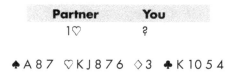

Partner	You
1♡	?

♠ A 8 7   ♡ K J 8 7 6   ◇ 3   ♣ K 10 5 4

Bid 4◇ , one level higher than a jump shift (3◇), showing a singleton diamond, primary trump support plus game-forcing values (13-16 support points).

*189. Although many play some form of splinter in response to a major-suit opening, not everyone does so in response to a minor-suit opening. The tip from here is to play them in both instances.

Partner	You
1◇	?

a)   ♠ 3   ♡ A 8 7   ◇ K Q 8 7 6 5   ♣ Q 10 9
b)   ♠ K J 10 9 8 7 4   ♡ 4   ◇ Q 3 2   ♣ 8 7

With (a), you should be thrilled that you can respond 3♠, a game force, to show this hand type.

With (b), you are annoyed that you cannot bid 3♠ to show this hand. Whenever you play a convention, you have to give up something. If you play that 3♠ is a splinter, then you must respond 1♠ with (b). Not playing splinters, respond 3♠.

190. A splinter response to a minor-suit opening bid denies a four-card major.

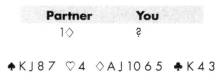

Partner	You
1◇	?

♠ K J 8 7   ♡ 4   ◇ A J 10 6 5   ♣ K 4 3

Respond 1♠. Do not splinter in hearts with an unbid four-card major.

191. A four-level splinter shows first- or second-round control in the unbid suit.

LHO	Partner	RHO	You
			1♠
2◇	2♡	pass	?

♠AKJ87 ♡AK76 ◇4 ♣976

Do not splinter to 4◇ without first- or second- round control in the unbid suit, clubs. Jump to 4♡ and hope for the best. A bid of 3♡ would not be forcing in this sequence: partner can have as little as 10-11 HCP to bid 2♡ in competition.

°192. After an opening bid of 1♣ or 1◇, when opener rebids a major suit at the one-level, jumps to the four-level by responder are splinter jumps.

Partner	You
1♣	1♡
1♠	?

♠KJ87 ♡AQJ65 ◇4 ♣K54

Jump to 4◇ to show the singleton diamond. A jump to 3◇ is natural. A jump to 4♣, partner's first suit, is also considered a splinter jump! Don't pull this one on partner without discussion!

193. When the opponents overcall, a jump in their suit by responder is a game-forcing splinter, showing a singleton, and jumping one level higher yet shows a void.

LHO	Partner	RHO	You
	1♣	1♡	?

a) ♠A87 ♡3 ◇J1054 ♣AK987
b) ♠A87 ♡— ◇K1054 ♣AQ9876

With (a), bid 3♡.
With (b), bid 4♡. You're in the fast lane now!

*194. When a splinter jump is doubled, a return to the trump suit is the weakest possible bid. A pass indicates further slam interest.

LHO	Partner	RHO	You
	1♣	pass	1♠
pass	3♡	dbl	?

a) ♠KJ543 ♡K94 ◇43 ♣876
b) ♠KQ543 ♡876 ◇QJ10 ♣Q10

With (a), return to 3♠, weak. You have wasted heart strength.

With (b), pass. You still have slam interest, but nothing to cuebid.

195. When a splinter jump is doubled, 'redouble' shows the ace of the splinter suit.

LHO	Partner	RHO	You
	1◇	pass	1♠
pass	3♡	dbl	?

♠KJ1087 ♡A876 ◇J4 ♣108

Redouble to show the ♡A.

BELOVED BLACKWOOD

196. Every 4NT bid is not Blackwood, and 'premature' Blackwood is not the best way to get to or stay out of many slams.

197. In most slam auctions, the stronger hand uses Blackwood. The weak hand tells; the strong hand asks. Reread this one.

198. Do not use Blackwood prematurely when you have two or more losers in an unbid suit.

Partner	You
1♣	1♠
3♣	?

♠ K Q 9 8 7   ♡ J 10 7   ◇ A K J 7   ♣ 2

Cuebid 4◇. Do not bid 4NT... yet. You have three quick losers in hearts, an unbid suit. You need a heart cuebid from partner before launching into Blackwood.

199. Do not use Blackwood prematurely with a void.

Partner	You
	2♣*
2◇*	2♠
3♠	?

♠ A K Q 8 7 6   ♡ —   ◇ K Q 8   ♣ A K Q 3

Cuebid 4♣, hoping for a 4◇ cuebid from partner. Rushing the net with a premature 4NT bid is losing bridge. Say partner does have one ace — how does that help when you don't know which one it is?

200. Do not ask partner for kings unless you have all four aces and the king of the agreed suit between the two hands. Partner is allowed to jump to seven in response to 5NT!

Playing Keycard Blackwood, do *not* bid 5NT unless you know that the combined hands have the four aces plus both the king and queen of the agreed suit. Partner is allowed to (encouraged to) jump to a grand slam after a 5NT ask if he can count thirteen tricks.

Partner	You
1♡	1♠
3♠	4NT
5♡	?

♠ K Q 10 8 7 6   ♡ 2   ◇ A Q J 4   ♣ K 4

Bid 6♠. Do not bid 5NT asking for kings. You are missing an ace. At duplicate bridge this rule about 5NT is sometimes waived in order to be able to play the hand in 6NT. Discuss this with your partner!

WHEN PARTNER BIDS BELOVED BLACKWOOD

201. Playing regular Blackwood as opposed to Keycard Blackwood, respond 5♣ with either no aces or all four aces. If partner can't tell the difference from the bidding, either you can't bid or partner can't play.

Note: If playing Keycard Blackwood, the king of the agreed suit counts as an ace. It is sometimes called 'Five Ace Blackwood'. If playing Roman Keycard Blackwood (RKCB), both the king and the queen of the agreed suit are included in the response. See Tips 492 and 493 for more on this topic.

202. Do not count a void as an ace.

203. With one ace (or three) plus a working void (not a void in partner's first-bid suit), jump to six of the void suit providing the void suit is lower-ranking than the trump suit. If the void suit is higher-ranking than the trump suit, jump to six of the trump suit.

Partner	You
1♡	4♡
4NT	?

a) ♠ — ♡ A J 4 3 2 ◇ J 10 8 7 6 ♣ J 8 7
b) ♠ J 10 8 7 6 ♡ A J 4 3 2 ◇ J 8 7 ♣ —

With (a), respond 6♡ to show one ace (or three) plus a higher-ranking void. (Do you think partner can work out where your void is?)

With (b), respond 6♣ to show one ace (or three) with a club void. As ever, your previous bidding determines whether you have one or three aces. Assuming the stronger hand bids Blackwood, the jump response will almost always show one ace.

204. With zero or two aces, plus a working void, respond 5NT. Only use 5NT with a void and zero aces if your previous bidding has shown a very weak hand. For practical purposes 5NT shows two aces (or keycards) and a void somewhere.

Partner	You
1♠	2♡
4NT	?

♠ 8 7 6   ♡ A J 10 8 7 6   ◇ —   ♣ A J 3 2

Respond 5NT to show two aces plus a void (which can't be in spades).

*205. If partner makes a four-level cuebid in your void suit, presumably showing the ace, and then bids 4NT, disregard the void and answer aces.

LHO	Partner	RHO	You
	1♠	2♡	2♠
3♡	4♡	pass	4♠
pass	4NT[1]	pass	?

1. Simple Blackwood.

♠ 10 9 4   ♡ —   ◇ A 8 7 6 5   ♣ J 10 8 7 6

Respond 5◇. Disregard the heart void: partner has cuebid the suit.

206. If the opponents mess with (interfere over) partner's Blackwood bid *below* the five-level of your agreed suit, double with no aces, pass with one ace, and bid the next-ranking suit with two aces, etc. This is called 'DOPI' (pronounced like the dwarf). 'D' stands for double; 'O' stands for zero; 'P' stands for pass; and 'I' stands for one.

LHO	Partner	RHO	You
	1♠	pass	3♠
4♡	4NT	5♡	?

♠ A 8 7 6   ♡ 8 7   ◇ K J 10 4   ♣ Q 5 4

Pass to show one ace, a DOPI response.

*207. If the opponents interfere with partner's Blackwood bid *above* the five-level of your agreed suit, double with an even number of aces (zero or two) pass with one ace; bid the next higher step with three aces. This convention is called 'DEPO'. **D**ouble-**E**ven, **P**ass-**O**dd.

LHO	Partner	RHO	You
			pass
pass	1♠	4♡	4♠
pass	4NT	6♣!	?

a) ♠ K J 8 7 ♡ 8 7 ◇ K Q 10 4 ♣ J 5 4
b) ♠ A 8 7 6 ♡ 8 7 ◇ K Q 10 4 ♣ J 5 4

With (a), double to show an even number of aces — zero! Double = Even number.

With (b), pass to show one ace. Pass = Odd number.

Playing Keycard Blackwood, the ♠K counts as an ace; you would pass with (a) to show an odd number of keycards.

208. If you can count thirteen tricks, do not answer kings. Bid the grand!

LHO	Partner	RHO	You
			4♡
4♠	4NT[1]	pass	5♣
pass	5NT	pass	?

1. Simple Blackwood. Playing Keycard Blackwood, the ♡K counts as an ace.

♠ 6 ♡ K Q 10 7 6 5 4 3 ◇ K Q 4 ♣ 4

Partner must have all four aces to bid 5NT. Bid seven. (See next tip.)

209. When you can count thirteen top tricks, bid 7NT, regardless of how good a fit you may have. In a suit contract, you run the risk of the opening lead being ruffed. In the previous example, bid 7NT, not 7♡.

210. If clubs or diamonds is the agreed suit and partner bids 4NT and then 5♠ over your response, bid 5NT. Don't worry, just do it! The hand is missing two aces and partner wants to get out at 5NT!

Partner	You
1♣	1♡
2♢	4♣
4NT	5♢
5♠	?

♠ 8 7   ♡ K Q 7 6 5   ♢ 4   ♣ A J 10 7 3

Bid 5NT. It is not for you to reason why; it is for you to do or die!

In the modern game after four-level game forcing club agreement, 4♢, not 4NT, is Keycard Blackwood. It saves space and avoids having to play 'lovely' contracts like 5NT when two aces are missing.

MORE SLAM BIDDING AIDS

211. When partner jumps to the five-level of the agreed major, he asks you to bid slam with first- or second-round control in the unbid suit.

Partner	You
	1◇
2♡	3♡
4♣	4◇
5♡	?

♠ Q J 4   ♡ J 7 6 5   ◇ A K J 8   ♣ Q 4

Partner's leap asks about spades, the unbid suit. You have neither first- nor second-round control. Pass.

212. If the opponents have bid one suit, a raise or leap to the five-level in the agreed major asks you to bid a slam with first- or second-round control in their suit.

LHO	Partner	RHO	You
			1♡
3♠	5♡	pass	?

♠ 8 7   ♡ K J 8 7 6 5   ◇ —   ♣ A K J 9 4

Pass. Partner is asking you about spades, the suit they have bid. You have neither first- nor second-round control in their suit. It's almost 100% that partner has a club void to justify this jump as he must have two quick spade losers.

213. Do not confuse the raise to the five-level in the agreed suit with a competitive bid at the five-level.

(a)

LHO	Partner	RHO	You
			1♡
4♠	5♡		

(b)

LHO	Partner	RHO	You
			1♡
2♠	3◇	3♠	4♡
pass	5♡		

In (a), 5♡ is competitive and does not ask about spades.

In (b), 5♡ is not competitive because your left-hand opponent has passed: this time, 5♡ asks about spades. The key is whether a *non-jump* raise comes after a pass or after a bid by the opponent. After a pass, it asks; after a bid, it does not.

214. When answering a five-level asking bid lacking first- or second-round control in the ask suit, pass. With the guarded king bid 5NT; with a singleton, bid six of the agreed suit; with the ace, cuebid their suit. With a void jump to a grand — just do it!

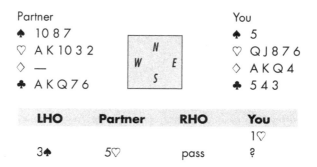

Partner		You
♠ 10 8 7		♠ 5
♡ A K 10 3 2		♡ Q J 8 7 6
◇ —		◇ A K Q 4
♣ A K Q 7 6		♣ 5 4 3

LHO	Partner	RHO	You
			1♡
3♠	5♡	pass	?

Bid 6♡, since you have a singleton spade. With the ♠A bid 5♠, with the ♠K bid 5NT, and with a spade void bid 7♡.

215. After partner makes a limit raise, do not even think about a slam unless you have a singleton or void.

Partner	You
	1♣
3♣	?

♠ A Q 3   ♡ K Q 5   ◇ K 4   ♣ A J 8 7 6

No singleton; no void; no slam! Bid 3NT.

216. Do not refuse a slam try when you have unexpectedly good trumps, regardless of outside strength. Jump in the trump suit.

Partner	You
1♡	3♡
3♠	?

♠ 7 6   ♡ A K Q 7 6   ◇ 8 7 6 5   ♣ 3 2

Bid 5♡. Partner is making a slam try with a terrible trump suit. Your jump shows great trumps, nothing else.

217. If notrump has not been bid previously, a leap to 5NT, the Grand Slam Force, asks a specific question: Which high honors do you have in our agreed suit? If there is no agreed suit, which honors do you have in the last bid suit?

(a)

Opener	Responder
1♡	5NT

(b)

Opener	Responder
1♣	1♠
3♠	5NT

In (a), responder asks about honors in hearts, the last bid suit.
In (b), responder asks about honors in spades, the agreed suit.

*218. When responding to the Grand Slam Force, these are the suggested responses:

6♣ The queen or less. If the queen is needed for seven, partner bids 6◇.

6◇ The ace or king and minimum length for your previous bidding.

6♡ The ace or king and maximum length for your previous bidding.

7♣ Two of the top three honors. Partner will convert to seven of the agreed suit or may convert to seven of a solid suit of his own.

219. In order to use the Grand Slam Force, you must be sure there are no losers in the side suits and you must have one of the top three honor cards in the trump suit.

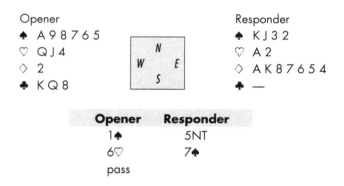

Opener		Responder
♠ A 9 8 7 6 5		♠ K J 3 2
♡ Q J 4		♡ A 2
◇ 2		◇ A K 8 7 6 5 4
♣ K Q 8		♣ —

Opener	Responder
1♠	5NT
6♡	7♠
pass	

Responder hauls out the trusty Grand Slam Force and opener responds 6♡, showing the ♠A or ♠K with extra length. Normal length would be five cards, so responder assumes six. Knowing of a ten-card spade fit, responder can bid the grand slam even though missing the queen.

*220. When clubs is the agreed suit, 4NT is a risky ace-ask. The response might easily push you beyond the safety level of 5♣. A better idea is to use a jump to 4◇, whether or not it was a previously bid suit, to ask for aces after clubs have been agreed at the three-level. It works!

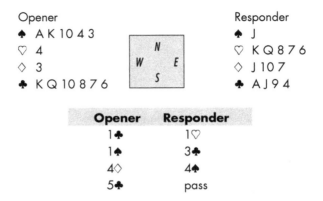

Opener	Responder
♠ A K 10 4 3	♠ J
♡ 4	♡ K Q 8 7 6
◇ 3	◇ J 10 7
♣ K Q 10 8 7 6	♣ A J 9 4

Opener	Responder
1♣	1♡
1♠	3♣
4◇	4♠
5♣	pass

What does it all mean? Well, 4◇ asks for aces and responder shows one. Opener, knowing two aces are missing, signs off in 5♣. Contrast this with the opener asking for aces via 4NT and getting a 5◇ response. Not so pretty. Keep in mind, you don't have to adopt every tip in this book. Just the good ones!

221. After an opening bid of 1NT or 2NT, a leap to 4♣ asks for aces (Gerber). To ask for kings, you subsequently bid 5♣. Gerber is generally used with long powerful suits, not balanced hands.

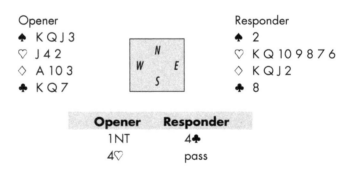

Opener	Responder
♠ K Q J 3	♠ 2
♡ J 4 2	♡ K Q 10 9 8 7 6
◇ A 10 3	◇ K Q J 2
♣ K Q 7	♣ 8

Opener	Responder
1NT	4♣
4♡	pass

Responder asks for aces via Gerber. Responses are by steps: 4◇ shows zero (or all four aces), 4♡ shows one ace, 4♠ shows two aces and 4NT shows three aces. Here, responder passes 4♡. The opponents have three aces!

222. Do not confuse Gerber leaps to 4♣ that come directly after bids of 1NT and 2NT with preemptive leaps to 4♣ or splinter jumps to 4♣ that show a singleton club.

a)	Partner	You		b)	Partner	You
	1♡	2♣				1♠
	4♣				2◇	2♠
					4♣	

c)	LHO	Partner	RHO	You
				1♣
	dbl	4♣		

(a) A strong raise in clubs. Partner has:

♠A4 ♡AQJ76 ◇32 ♣AQ87

(b) A splinter jump showing a singleton club. Partner has:

♠A76 ♡654 ◇AK7643 ♣5

(c) Long clubs and a weak distributional hand. Partner has:

♠5 ♡94 ◇K932 ♣Q108764

223. If the Gerber bidder bids 4NT after receiving a response to 4♣, he is not making an 'honesty check' by re-asking for aces. He is saying that he wants to play the hand in 4NT — two aces are missing!

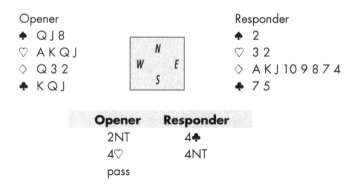

Opener
♠ QJ8
♡ AKQJ
◇ Q32
♣ KQJ

Responder
♠ 2
♡ 32
◇ AKJ109874
♣ 75

Opener	Responder
2NT	4♣
4♡	4NT
pass	

Responder checks for aces, and once again, finds that two are missing. Rather than play at the five-level in diamonds, responder opts to play at the four-level in notrump.

224. Bid conservatively with 'aceless wonders'. Bid aggressively with solid suits.

Partner	You
	1♣
1◇	?

     a)   ♠ K Q 4   ♡ K Q   ◇ 2   ♣ K J 10 8 7 5 4
     b)   ♠ A 10 4   ♡ 4 3   ◇ 2   ♣ A K Q 10 8 7 6

With (a), rebid 2♣. Avoid making jump rebids with aceless wonders.
     With (b), rebid 3♣.

225. After you open 1NT or 2NT and partner invites with 4NT, pass with a minimum. If you have a maximum with a four-card minor or a five-card major, bid that suit at the five-level. If you have a maximum with a five-card minor, jump to the six-level in that suit. Partner either passes or converts to 6NT.

Partner	You
	1NT
4NT	?

♠ K 6 5 2   ♡ A 9 8   ◇ A Q 6 5   ♣ A 7

Bid 5◇ to show a maximum, plus a four-card diamond suit. If partner also has four diamonds, the hand should play easier in diamonds than notrump. (See next tip.)

226. There is no bridge law stating that you must use Blackwood in order to arrive at a slam. Two balanced hands facing each other seldom use Blackwood.

Opener		Responder
♠ K 6 5 2		♠ A 8
♡ A 9 8		♡ K Q 4
◇ A Q 6 5		◇ K J 3 2
♣ A 7		♣ K 8 4 3

Opener	Responder
1NT	4NT
5◇	6◇
pass	

These two hands have a combined count of 33 HCP, but there are only eleven notrump tricks. If diamonds are trumps, you should make 6◇ easily and have a good chance to take all the tricks! This illustrates the advantage of playing a 4-4 fit.

227. With 34-36 HCP between two balanced hands, bid 6NT in preference to a 4-4 fit. The contract usually makes on power and you don't have to sweat out a bad trump division.

THINKING OF PREEMPTING?

228. Do not open with a beneath-game preempt holding two aces or one ace and two kings. You have too much defensive strength.

229. Vul. vs. not, your suit should contain three of the top five honors.

230. After you preempt and partner bids a new suit beneath the game level, you cannot pass!

Partner	You
	3♡
4♣	?

♠ 3　♡ K J 10 9 8 7 4　◇ Q J 9　♣ 10 2

Whatever you do, don't pass! Partner's 4♣ is forcing. Try 4♡; your hearts look pretty good.

231. After you make a three-level minor-suit preempt, try to show a side stopper below 3NT if partner makes a forcing response.

Partner	You
	3♣
3◇	?

♠ Q J 4　♡ 3 2　◇ 2　♣ A J 10 8 7 6 4

Bid 3♠ to show a spade stopper. You can't have a spade suit (see next tip).

232. Do not make a preemptive opening bid in a minor with a side four-card major.

♠ K Q 5 4　♡ 3　◇ 2　♣ A 10 9 8 7 6 5

As dealer, pass. You have a four card major.

233. Do not preempt in one major holding four cards in the other... unless your suit can play easily opposite a singleton.

a) ♠A 10 8 7 6 5 4 ♡K 5 4 3 ◇2 ♣9

b) ♠A K J 10 9 3 2 ♡J 10 9 8 ◇3 ♣5

With (a), pass. Your long suit is not independent and preempting in spades may lose a heart fit.

With (b), open 4♠ at any vulnerability. Your spades are so strong that it won't matter if you miss a heart fit. With 7-4 bid some more! See next tip.

234. Do not open with a three-bid if your hand qualifies for an opening four-bid. Most hands with eight-card suits or 7-4 distribution open four as opposed to three.

a) ♠A Q J 10 7 6 4 ♡3 ◇Q J 9 3 ♣3

b) ♠K Q J 9 8 7 6 5 ♡3 ◇4 ♣Q 10 9

Both of these hands open 4♠, not 3♠.

235. Position is important when preempting. First- and second-seat preempts show traditional values; third-seat preempts are suspect because partner has already passed and the preemptive bidder is allowed to stretch to direct the opening lead. Fourth-seat preempts are the next thing to opening bids. With a weak hand in fourth seat, pass the hand out.

♠3 ♡K 5 4 ◇K J 10 8 7 6 4 ♣J 7

Open 3◇ in first, second or third seat; pass in fourth seat.

236. A fourth-seat opening of 3♣ or 3◇ invites partner to bid 3NT. The opener shows a solid suit.

♠4 ♡6 5 4 ◇A K Q 10 5 3 2 ♣K 4

In first, second or third seat, open 1◇. In fourth seat, open 3◇.

237. A response of 3NT to a three-level preemptive opening ends the auction.

Partner	You
	3♡
3NT	?

♠ 10 7   ♡ Q J 10 8 7 6 5   ◇ K J 5   ♣ 3

Pass. It's no longer on your head. Partner could have solid clubs with a heart void!

238. Preempt as often as possible consistent with the vulnerability. Preempts drive the opponents mad.

239. After you preempt, partner is in charge and makes the sacrifices, not you! Reread this one.

Not vul. vs. vul.:

LHO	Partner	RHO	You
			3♡
3♠	4♡	4♠	?

♠ 4   ♡ K Q J 9 7 6 2   ◇ J 10 9   ♣ 8 7

Even thinking of bidding 5♡ is an overbid! Pass. Your hand is known, but partner's is not. What about the vulnerability? Partner knows about that, too, and may be frothing at the mouth to double.

240. When you make a preemptive bid and then double an eventual contract (usually a slam), it generally indicates a side-suit void. The double forbids the lead of your suit and asks (begs) partner to find your void suit.
   You hold:

♠ A J 10 9 7 4 2   ♡ 6 4 3   ◇ —   ♣ J 10 7

LHO	Partner	RHO	You
			3♠
4♡	pass	4NT	pass
5♡	pass	6♡	?

Double and pray partner has heard of this tip!

241. Say you open 3♡ and partner raises to 5♡. What does it mean? It means partner wants to play in 6♡ if your trump suit can play for one loser opposite a small doubleton.

LHO	Partner	RHO	You
			3♠
pass	5♠	pass	?

a) ♠ Q J 10 9 8 7 6   ♡ —   ◇ K J 8   ♣ 4 3 2
b) ♠ K Q J 8 7 6 5   ♡ 4 3   ◇ 4 3   ♣ 3 2

With (a), pass. You have two trump losers.
　　With (b), bid 6♠. You have one trump loser.

242. After you open 4♡ or 4♠ and partner raises to the five-level, partner is asking you to bid six if your suit can play opposite a singleton for one loser. If it can't, pass.

LHO	Partner	RHO	You
			4♠
pass	5♠	pass	?

a) ♠ Q J 10 9 8 7 4 3   ♡ —   ◇ K Q 5   ♣ 8 7
b) ♠ K Q J 9 6 4 3 2   ♡ 2   ◇ 5 4   ♣ 6 5

With (a), pass. You have the same two trump losers.
　　With (b), bid 6♠. You should be off the ♠A, period.

WHEN THEY PREEMPT

243. Be aggressive over enemy preempts with a singleton in their suit. Double with as few as 12 HCP with 4-4-4-1 distribution. With a doubleton in the opponent's suit, look at your support for the unbid major(s). With four-card support, double with as few as 14 HCP; with three-card support, double with 15+ HCP.

LHO	Partner	RHO	You
		3♡	?

a) ♠A J 10 4   ♡5   ◇K J 10 4   ♣K 10 8 7
b) ♠Q 8 4 2   ♡3 2   ◇K Q 8 4   ♣A K 3
c) ♠Q 8 4   ♡3 2   ◇A J 9 8   ♣A Q 9 4

With (a) or (b), double. With (c), pass.

244. Assume partner has between 4-8 HCP when considering a bid over an enemy preempt. If you don't, you will be afraid to compete. And if he doesn't have that much, get a new partner who does.

245. An overcall of a preemptive bid shows opening bid values. A jump over a preempt is strong. When the bid to your right is weak, a jump by you is strong. With a preemptive hand of your own, pass for the time being.

LHO	Partner	RHO	You
		3♣	?

a) ♠A Q 10 9 4 3   ♡A 2   ◇Q J 6   ♣4 3
b) ♠A K J 10 7 2   ♡2   ◇A Q J 9   ♣3 2
c) ♠K Q 10 8 5 4 2   ♡4 2   ◇Q 6   ♣8 7

With (a), bid 3♠.
    With (b), bid 4♠.
    With (c), pass.

246. A sensible defense to three-level preempts is to play that 'double' shows a three-suited hand, a cuebid shows a two-suited hand, and bidding or jumping in a suit shows a one-suited hand.

247. If your right-hand opponent opens 3♣ or 3◇, a cuebid of 4♣ or 4◇ is a takeout for the majors. It shows 5-5 or 6-5 distribution with a hand you would have opened.

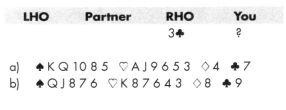

LHO	Partner	RHO	You
		3♣	?

  a)   ♠K Q 10 8 5   ♡A J 9 6 5 3   ◇4   ♣7
  b)   ♠Q J 8 7 6   ♡K 8 7 6 4 3   ◇8   ♣9

With (a), bid 4♣.
    With (b), pass.

248. If your right-hand opponent opens 3♡, overcall 4♡ to show spades plus an unknown minor. This cuebid shows 5-5 or 5-6 (five cards in the major and six in the minor) with opening bid values.

LHO	Partner	RHO	You
		3♡	?

     ♠A J 10 4 3   ♡3   ◇A K J 7 4 3   ♣3

Bid 4♡. Partner bids 4NT to ask for your minor.

    Bid the same way after a 3♠ opening bid. A cuebid of 4♠ shows five hearts and a likely six-card minor with a whale of a hand! After all, you have forced the bidding to the five-level! Partner bids 4NT to discover your minor.

249. The double of an opening 4♡ bid is takeout oriented. The doubler must have at least three spades. A direct overcall of 4NT shows the minors: it is not Blackwood.

LHO	Partner	RHO	You
		4♡	?

a) ♠A2 ♡KQ5 ◇A8765 ♣Q98
b) ♠A32 ♡4 ◇KQ87 ♣AK653
c) ♠3 ♡5 ◇AJ876 ♣AQ10752

With (a), pass. Don't double. Look at your spades! How thrilled will you be to hear 4♠?

With (b), double.

With (c), overcall 4NT.

*250. How should you deal with an opening 4♠ bid? Good question. The tip from here is to double with either a three-suited hand short in spades or a strong balanced hand. Overcall 4NT to show a wild two-suiter, and cuebid 5♠ to show an 'end-of-the-world' three-suiter. Do *not* double simply because you have spade strength. Pass with strong spades and hope partner reopens with a double. Best is for either you or your partner to open 4♠ and let them deal with it.

LHO	Partner	RHO	You
		4♠	?

a) ♠4 ♡AQ76 ◇KQ54 ♣AK32
b) ♠AK92 ♡3 ◇A765 ♣J1043
c) ♠543 ♡AK7 ◇AQ4 ♣AJ94
d) ♠— ♡KQ876 ◇AQJ987 ♣K2
e) ♠4 ♡3 ◇KQ1087 ♣AKJ654
f) ♠— ♡AKJ4 ◇AQJ87 ♣AKQ4

With (a), double.

With (b), pass. It only hurts for a little while.

With (c), double.

With (d), bid 4NT. If partner bids 5♣, bid 5◇ to show the red suits.

With (e), bid 4NT. This time you have the minors.

With (f), bid 5♠. Don't worry; you'll never hold this hand, but it was fun making it up!

251. When partner doubles a game preempt, pass with most balanced hands, remove the double with distributional hands.

LHO	Partner	RHO	You
4♡	dbl	pass	?

a) ♠A76 ♡543 ◇QJ54 ♣Q108
b) ♠A76 ♡543 ◇QJ8765 ♣3

With (a), pass.
　　With (b), bid 5◇.

252. The time to become aggressive is when a three-level preempt is passed around to you and you have a singleton in the opponent's suit with support for the other suits. Double with as little as 10 HCP. With a doubleton in the opponent's suit and support for the unbid major(s), double with as few as 11 or 12 HCP. With three cards in their suit, you need 15-16 HCP to reopen with a double.

LHO	Partner	RHO	You
3♡	pass	pass	?

a) ♠AJ92 ♡43 ◇QJ76 ♣K87
b) ♠AJ5 ♡632 ◇Q876 ♣AQ4
c) ♠AJ98 ♡5 ◇KQ87 ♣J976

With (a), double.
　　With (b), pass.
　　With (c), double.

253. Are you ready for this one? An overcall of 3NT after a three-level opening bid has a range of 16-22 HCP!

LHO	Partner	RHO	You
		3♠	?

a) ♠AQ ♡Q87 ◇AQJ9 ♣J1087
b) ♠AKJ ♡A87 ◇KQ76 ♣AJ2

Overcall 3NT with both hands! How will partner know? He won't!
Assume partner has 18-19 HCP if this sequence comes up.

254. Preemptive opening bids with very light hands are all the rage these days. Be prepared for three-level preempts on six-card suits, etc. Third-seat non-vulnerable preemptive three-bids tend to be light. Forewarned is forearmed.

255. The modern defense to weak opening bids of 2♡ *or* 2♠ is Leaping Michaels! And just what is that? It is a leap to 4♣ or 4◇ to show a powerful two-suited hand with five cards in the other major and five, usually six, cards in the bid minor. The bid is not forcing, but it takes next to nothing to bid game in either suit. Look at the examples to see what Leaping Michaels looks like.

LHO	Partner	RHO	You
		2♡	?

a) ♠ A Q J 6 5 ♡ 5 ◇ A K J 10 8 4 ♣ 3
b) ♠ K Q J 6 5 ♡ A ◇ 4 ♣ A J 10 8 6 4

With (a), leap to 4◇.

With (b), leap to 4♣.

When you play Leaping Michaels, the direct cuebid of opener's suit (here 3♡) shows a solid minor and asks partner to bid 3NT with a heart stopper. You might have:

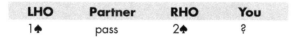

♠ K 4 ♡ 5 2 ◇ A K Q J 6 5 4 ♣ A 8

If partner doesn't have a heart stopper, you will wind up in diamonds. Leaping Michaels is also 'on' after this start:

LHO	Partner	RHO	You
1♠	pass	2♠	?

A jump to 4♣ or 4◇ by you shows a huge two-suited hand with five hearts and five or six cards in the bid minor. A cuebid of 3♠ shows a solid minor and asks partner to bid 3NT with a spade stopper. Now you are ready for anything!

When partner makes a cuebid asking you to bid 3NT with a stopper in the opponent's suit, you may not have a stopper! If you don't, and you can't be sure which minor partner has, bid 4♣ with a weak hand and 5♣ with a strong hand. Partner will correct to diamonds if necessary.

WHEN YOU ARE A PASSED HAND

256. A new suit response to an opening bid is not forcing. If you wish to force, jump shift. A jump shift is a one-round force, not a game force.

*257. A jump shift promises primary trump support for opener's suit. It does not show an 'almost opening bid'. It can be made on a four-card suit.

Partner	You
	pass
1♣	?

a) ♠ A K 8 7 6 ♡ K 8 7 ◊ J 7 6 ♣ 3 2
b) ♠ A K J 4 ♡ 4 ◊ 4 3 ♣ Q 10 8 7 6 5

With (a), bid 1♠. A jump to 2♠ promises at least five clubs.
   With (b), bid 2♠.

258. A jump response to an overcall shows a two-suited hand — the suit you are bidding and partner's suit. It is called a **fit-showing jump**.

LHO	Partner	RHO	You
			pass
1♡	2♣	2♡	?

♠ K Q 10 4 3 ♡ 2 ◊ 5 4 ♣ A 10 8 7 6

Bid 3♠ to show a spade-club two-suiter.

*259. A jump response that is one level higher than a jump shift is a splinter jump.

Partner	You
	pass
1◇	?

♠ A 5 4   ♡ 3   ◇ Q J 8 7 6 5   ♣ K 4 2

Bid 3♡. Your jump shows a massive diamond fit, a singleton heart, and 9-11 HCP. Perfect. With a preempt in hearts, you would have opened 3♡.

260. A direct overcall of 1NT after a major-suit opening bid is 'unusual' for the minors. It shows 5-5 or 6-5 either way with 7-10 HCP.

LHO	Partner	RHO	You
			pass
pass	pass	1♠	?

♠ 4   ♡ 5   ◇ Q J 8 7 6   ♣ A Q 7 6 5 3

Bid 1NT. If you are a *non-passed* hand, the jump to 2NT shows the minors and a 1NT overcall is natural.

261. A 1NT overcall of a minor-suit opening bid is also 'unusual.' It shows *five hearts* plus five or six cards in the other minor with 7-10 HCP.

LHO	Partner	RHO	You
			pass
pass	pass	1◇	?

♠ 4   ♡ K 10 7 6 5   ◇ 5   ♣ A 10 9 6 5 4

Overcall 1NT to show the two lower-ranking unbid suits, hearts and clubs.

262. There is no such animal as a *direct* overcall of 1NT to show a balanced hand. All *direct* notrump overcalls are unusual.

LHO	Partner	RHO	You
			pass
pass	pass	1♡	?

♠ A 10 4   ♡ K J 9   ◇ Q 10 4 2   ♣ J 9 8

Pass. Do not even think of bidding 1NT. You would be showing a minor two-suiter!

263. *Balancing* 1NT bids are *natural* and show 10-12 HCP — more often 10-11 HCP as many balanced 12 HCP hands open.

LHO	Partner	RHO	You
			pass
1♡	pass	pass	?

♠ A 10 4   ♡ K J 9   ◇ Q 10 4 2   ♣ J 9 8

Reopen with 1NT, natural. You are in the balancing seat.

264. A balancing 2NT bid is 'unusual.' After a major-suit opening, it shows the minors. After a minor-suit opening, it shows hearts plus the other minor, 7-10 HCP.

265. Avoid a two-level response on a four-card suit like the plague. Partner may pass with a small doubleton in your suit. You will not be a happy camper playing a 4-2 fit.

Partner	You
	pass
1♡	?

♠ 3 2   ♡ K J 5   ◇ A K 8 7   ♣ 5 4 3 2

Assuming you don't play Drury (an artificial response of 2♣ showing 10-12 with three- or four-card support for opener's major), respond 3♡ rather than 2◇. The risk of being dropped in 2◇ is greater than the one trump you owe partner for your jump. (See Tip 485.)

266. A 2NT response shows 11-12 balanced and denies a singleton. A one- or two-level response followed by 2NT shows the same strength but may contain a singleton.

Partner	You
	pass
1♠	?

a) ♠76 ♡AJ5 ◇KJ43 ♣Q1054
b) ♠7 ♡AJ43 ◇KJ4 ♣Q8765

With (a), respond 2NT. With (b), respond 2♣ and rebid 2NT if partner rebids 2♠ or 2◇. If you are playing Drury (see Tip 485), you have a messy problem with this hand.

267. There is no such animal as a natural response of 3NT unless you mis- sorted your hand or miscounted your points.

268. With 4-4-4-1 shape, double with as few as 9 HCP if the opponents open your short suit.

LHO	Partner	RHO	You
			pass
pass	pass	1♡	?

a) ♠KJ43 ♡5 ◇K1054 ♣Q976
b) ♠KJ43 ♡65 ◇K876 ♣Q76
c) ♠KJ3 ♡J654 ◇A876 ♣Q8

With (a), double. With (b), double.

With (c), pass — four-cards in their suit means no takeout double for this hand!

269. With any 4-4-3-2 distribution, double with 9-11 HCP if your right- hand opponent opens in your short suit. Otherwise, double if you have at least four-card support for both unbid majors. If neither of these options exist, make the best bid in bridge — 'pass'!

270. After an intervening overcall, a cuebid substitutes for the limit raise. The jump raise becomes preemptive. This idea is both popular and effective.

LHO	Partner	RHO	You
			pass
pass	1♡	2♣	?

a) ♠ 8 7 ♡ K 10 8 7 ◇ Q 10 5 4 2 ♣ 3 2
b) ♠ 8 7 ♡ A Q 8 7 ◇ K J 10 4 ♣ J 3 2

With (a), bid 3♡, preemptive.
  With (b), bid 3♣, a limit raise in hearts.

AFTER PARTNER OPENS 1NT

*271. Do not use Stayman with 4=3=3=3 or 3=4=3=3 distribution. There are more upsides than downsides to playing in notrump on flat hands.

272. You usually need at least 9 HCP to use Stayman, but 8 HCP will suffice if you have both majors. If you do not connect in a major and are forced to retreat to 2NT, partner will play you for 9 HCP.

Partner	You
1NT	?

a) ♠A876 ♡Q753 ◇53 ♣1065
b) ♠AJ43 ♡K1043 ◇43 ♣987

With (a), pass. You are not strong enough to launch into a Stayman sequence. Partner may rebid 2◇, then what?

   With (b), bid 2♣ looking at 8 HCP with both majors. If partner rebids 2◇, rebid 2NT without being ashamed of your dummy.

273. With a three-suited hand short in clubs, you can even use Stayman with a bust. You are planning to pass any rebid partner makes, including 2◇.

Partner	You
1NT	?

♠Q1054 ♡J987 ◇109876 ♣—

Bid 2♣ and pass anything partner bids.

*274. If RHO overcalls at the two-level, some play that a three-level cuebid is Stayman, others play that 'double' is Stayman, others that double is for penalty. Still others use 2NT as a transfer to 3♣ followed by a cuebid as Stayman. Finally, many play that 2NT is a transfer to 3♣ and then cuebidding the opponent's suit is Stayman without a stopper, and bidding 3NT is Stayman with a stopper. Help! Pick out what best suits your partnership but definitely discuss this sequence!

LHO	Partner	RHO	You
	1NT	2♡	?

♠ K 8 7 6   ♡ 3 2   ◇ J 5 4   ♣ A Q 9 8

Since you want to use Stayman, fall back on your agreement. Either bid 3♡ directly or bid 2NT followed by 3♡ or 3NT, or double. Just have an agreement! One that you both remember! Write it down!

*275. If your right-hand opponent makes a three-level overcall, 'double' replaces Stayman. If you wish to make a penalty double, you can't; either pass or bid 3NT. You can't have your cake and eat it too.

LHO	Partner	RHO	You
	1NT	3♡	?

a) ♠ A J 4 3   ♡ 4 2   ◇ K 10 7 5   ♣ Q 4 3
b) ♠ 7 5   ♡ K J 9 3   ◇ 4 3   ♣ J 8 7 6 5

With (a), double (Stayman). Partner can either bid 3♠ with four spades, pass with good hearts or bid 3NT. With (b), pass. Sorry.

276. If you are not using transfer responses to notrump opening bids, reconsider. It is important that the stronger of the two hands be the declarer. In addition, you have many follow-up options that are not available if you don't use transfers.

277. If your opponents play that a double of partner's 1NT opening bid shows an *unknown* one-suited hand, ignore the double and play as if the double never happened. System is 'on' (2♣ is Stayman, etc.).

278. If your opponents play that an overcall of 2♣ shows an *unknown* one-suiter, double is Stayman and everything else retains its original meaning.

*279. If your opponents play that a double of 1NT is for penalty, try this escape method with weak hands:

» Redouble to force partner to bid 2♣ and then pass or bid 2◊ to get out in either of those suits.

» 2♣ is still Stayman and can be used with 5-4 or 4-5 in the majors and a relatively weak hand. (0-6 HCP). If partner bids 2◊, bid your five-card major.

» 2◊ and 2♡ are transfers, and 2NT is how you escape with weak hand with at least 5-5 in the minors.

» A jump to the three-level in a minor suit shows a six or seven card suit and a very weak hand. Something like:

♠ 5   ♡ 5 4   ◊ 9 8 4   ♣ Q J 8 7 4 3 2

280. If the opponents play that a double of 1NT is for penalty, pass with any weak balanced hand lacking a five-card suit. Don't try to find a home that may not exist. See the previous tip for how to get out with weak hands and long suits.

281. Playing a 15-17 1NT range, do not open 1NT with 17 HCP and any reasonable five-card suit (headed by any two honor cards). Treat the hand as an 18-pointer and open the five-card suit.

282. A direct raise to 4NT is natural; a 2♣ response followed by 4NT is also natural.

Partner	You
1NT	?

a)   ♠ A J   ♡ Q 10 4   ◊ K 8 7 6 5   ♣ A J 10
b)   ♠ A J   ♡ Q 10 4 2   ◊ K 8 7 6   ♣ A Q 5

With (a), bid 4NT.

With (b), bid 2♣. If partner rebids 2◊ or 2♠, rebid 4NT, natural.

*283. After a Stayman ask and a *major*-suit response from partner, a jump to 4♣ is keycard for the major, a jump to 4NT is natural. This jump agrees partner's major and asks for aces (or keycards). This is one of the only times that 4♣ is used to ask for aces when the previous bid is not 1NT or 2NT.

Partner	You
1NT	2♣
2♠	?

♠K Q 7 6   ♡4   ♢K Q 7 6 5   ♣K J 9

Jump to 4♣ to ask for aces (or keycards).

284. With a six-card minor headed by two of the top three honors and 7-11 HCP, leap to 3NT. Do not bother showing the minor suit. In both cases you have 'notrump suits'. These are suits that almost always take the same number of tricks in notrump as they will in a suit contract.

Partner	You
1NT	?

a) ♠4   ♡8 7 6   ♢A K J 8 7 3   ♣4 3 2
b) ♠J 4   ♡3 2   ♢7 6 5   ♣A Q J 6 5 2

Raise to 3NT on both hands.

285. The following two-part tip presumes you play two- and four-level major suit transfers. (4♢ is to 4♡ and 4♡ is to 4♠).

285A. With a five-card major and a balanced type hand, make a two-level transfer and pass with 0-7 HCP, raise to 2NT with 8-9 HCP, raise to 3NT with 10-15 HCP and leap to 4NT with 16-17 HCP, not Blackwood. 4NT can be passed.

a) ♠A Q 8 4 3   ♡K 2   ♢J 4 3   ♣K J 10
b) ♠A Q 8 4 3   ♡K 2   ♢A 4 3   ♣Q J 9

With a) bid 2♡ and then 3NT.
   With b) bid 2♡ and then 4NT.

285B. With a six-card major, transfer at the two-level and then pass with 0-5 HCP, raise to the three-level with 6-8 HCP and raise to the four-level with 13-15 HCP, a slam try. With 8-12 HCP make a four-level transfer and either pass or ask for keycards by bidding 4NT.

   a) ♠ 2 ♡ K J 9 8 4 3 ◇ K J 3 ♣ 10 8 7
   b) ♠ A Q J 7 4 3 ♡ 2 ◇ K Q 10 3 ♣ K 4

With a) bid 4◇, a transfer to 4♡, and then pass.

 With b) bid 4♡, a transfer to 4♠, and then bid 4NT, Keycard Blackwood.

 I might add that on the list of memorable disasters is one hand bidding 4♡ as a transfer to 4♠ and partner passing. Playing a 2-1 fit builds character and leads to interesting post-mortems.

286. If you have 5-4 or 4-5 in the majors with game-going strength (9+ HCP), respond 2♣. If partner bids 2◇, jump to the three-level in your *four-card major.* This allows partner to play the hand when holding three cards in your five-card major. If you bid your five-card major first and partner supports, the weaker hand is the declarer. This convention is called **Smolen** and enjoys great popularity among experts. This convention can also be used when responding to 2NT with this distribution. After you bid 3♣ and partner bids 3◇, bid your four-card major.

AFTER PARTNER RESPONDS 2♣ TO YOUR OPENING 1NT BID

*287. If you believe in opening 1NT with a five-card major or a six-card minor, bid your suit at the three-level, with a jump if necessary, to let partner in on the secret.

Partner	You
	1NT
2♣	?

a)   ♠A 2 ♡A Q 10 5 4 ♢K 7 5 ♣K 4 2
b)   ♠K 2 ♡K 2 ♢A Q 8 7 6 5 ♣K 10 7

With (a), bid 3♡. With (b), bid 3♢.

288. With no four-card major, bid 2♢. Do *not* bid 2NT to show a maximum.

*289. With two four-card majors, bid hearts first.

Partner	You
	1NT
2♣	?

♠A Q J 7 ♡J 10 4 3 ♢A Q 4 ♣K 7

Bid 2♡. If partner bids 3NT, bid 4♠. Partner must have four spades.

*290. If your right-hand opponent doubles 2♣, showing long, strong clubs:

» Bid a four-card major if you have one.
» If you do not have a four-card major but do have a club stopper, pass.
» If you do not have a four-card major and you don't have a club stopper, bid 2◇.
» If you have four or five wonderful clubs, redouble.

LHO	Partner	RHO	You
			1NT
pass	2♣	dbl	?

a) ♠ A J 8 7 ♡ K 8 7 ◇ A 9 8 ♣ A 8 7
b) ♠ A J 9 ♡ K 7 6 ◇ A K J 3 ♣ 8 7 6
c) ♠ A J 9 ♡ K 7 6 ◇ K J 4 3 ♣ A 8 7
d) ♠ A 10 ♡ K 7 6 ◇ A J 4 ♣ Q J 9 8 7

With (a), bid 2♠.

With (b), bid 2◇ — no four-card major, no club stopper.

With (c), pass — no four-card major, but a club stopper.

With (d), redouble. You are more than willing to play 2♣ doubled and redoubled.

FOUR NOTRUMP

291. A bid of 4NT is not always Blackwood. Wait, don't burn this book! A bid of 4NT can be Blackwood, it can be a takeout for the minors, it can be a three-suited takeout, it can be a two-suited takeout or it can be natural. It all depends upon the previous bidding. Now you can burn the book.

292. After either player bids 1NT or 2NT, and is raised by partner to 4NT, the 4NT bid is natural and not forcing. To ask for aces in these sequences, jump to 4♣, Gerber. If you don't use Gerber, now is a good time to start.

293. After a bid of the *fourth* suit by either the opener or the responder, 4NT is natural. The range is 17-19 HCP.

a)
Opener	Responder
1♠	2◇
2♡	3♣¹
4NT²	

b)
Opener	Responder
1◇	1♡
2◇	2♠
3♣¹	4NT²

1. Fourth suit.
2. Natural.

294. After a 1NT rebid by the opener, a leap to 4NT by the responder is natural.

Opener	Responder
1◇	1♡
1NT	4NT

Here, 4NT is invitational showing 19 HCP. To ask for aces, you must leap to 4♣, Gerber. See Tip 221.

*295. After a two-over-one response and a 3NT rebid by opener, 4NT by responder is natural.

Opener	Responder
1♠	2◇
3NT	4NT[1]

1. Natural.

Since 4♣ is also natural by responder in this auction, in the absence of more sophisticated agreements, leap to 5♣ (**Super Gerber**) over 3NT to ask for aces.

296. When neither you nor your partner has bid previously and the opponents are bidding one or both majors, 4NT by either you or partner is for the minors.

a)

LHO	Partner	RHO	You
1♡	pass	3♡/4♡	4NT

b)

LHO	Partner	RHO	You
2♡[1]	pass	4♠	4NT

1. Weak.

c)

LHO	Partner	RHO	You
		4♡	4NT

All of the 4NT bids are takeouts for the minors.

297. After partner opens 1♣ or 1◇ and second hand overcalls 4♠, 4NT is for takeout.

LHO	Partner	RHO	You
	1♣	4♠	?

a) ♠4 ♡KQ87 ◇AQ975 ♣AJ9
b) ♠4 ♡AJ1065 ◇AK7654 ♣4

Bid 4NT on both hands. If partner bids 5♣, pass with (a); bid 5◇ with (b) to show diamonds and hearts. No Blackwood after a minor-suit opening and a 4♠ overcall.

298. Here's a dynamite tip: Use an opening bid of 4NT to ask for specific aces. With no aces, partner responds 5♣; with one ace, partner bids the suit in which the ace is held. Holding the ♣A, partner responds 6♣. With two aces (don't hold your breath), partner responds 5NT. This opening bid is reserved for powerful freak hands that contain a void — for example:

♠ A K Q 9 8 5 4 3   ♡ K Q J 2   ◇ A   ♣ —

Open 4NT! If partner responds 5♡, bid 7♠. If partner responds 5NT, bid 7NT. If partner responds 5♣ or 6♣, sign off in 6♠. Don't expect to use this opening bid very often.

WHEN YOU MAKE A NEGATIVE DOUBLE

299. Negative doubles do not follow all-inclusive rules. What they show depends upon the level and which major suits are unbid.

300. You can only make a negative double as the *responder*, and it must be made at your first opportunity. As a result, you cannot make an immediate penalty double after any one-, two-, or three-level overcall.

301. In theory, a negative double tends to deny a six-card major.

302. Doubling and then bidding a major suit almost always shows a five-card suit. Doubling and then bidding a minor suit can show either a five- or a six-card suit.

LHO	Partner	RHO	You
	1♣	1♠	dbl
pass	2♣	pass	2♦

♠ 8 7 6   ♡ A 7 6 5   ♦ K 10 9 8 4 3   ♣ —

Your 2♦ bid after partner has rebid his suit typically shows four hearts, six diamonds and a hand not strong enough to bid 2♦ directly in competition, which shows 10+ HCP. With a doubleton club and five diamonds you would normally pass 2♣ and you might even pass with a singleton club looking at five or six shabby diamonds.

303. Negative doubles at the one- and two-levels with five- and six-card suits are limited. They show a maximum of 10 HCP. With more bid the long suit directly. Think of a negative double followed by a new suit as trying to put brakes on the bidding sequence.

*304. A negative double of a 1♡ overcall promises four spades. Bidding 1♠ shows at least five spades.

LHO	Partner	RHO	You
	1♣/1◇	1♡	dbl

You promise exactly four spades. A 1♠ response shows at least five spades.
Note: some play that a double in this sequence *denies* four spades.

305. Negative doubles with four-card suits are unlimited. At the one-level, they promise a minimum of 6 'working' HCP. See Tip 311. However, holding 11+ HCP with a five-card minor and four cards in the unbid major, forget the negative double as you are strong enough to bid both suits starting with the minor. If you double and then bid the minor, you will not be showing that strong a hand.

306. When both minors have been bid at the one-level, 'double' promises four cards in each of the unbid majors or possibly five hearts and four spades with 6-9 HCP.

LHO	Partner	RHO	You
	1♣	1◇	?

a) ♠AJ87 ♡KQ76 ◇54 ♣A76
b) ♠AJ87 ♡K43 ◇543 ♣987
c) ♠AJ965 ♡KQ76 ◇43 ♣32
d) ♠AQ32 ♡108765 ◇43 ♣J6

With (a), double. You have four cards in each unbid major.

With (b), bid 1♠.

With (c), bid 1♠. No negative doubles with five-card spade suits at the one-level.

With (d), double. If you respond 1♡, you may lose a spade fit if fourth hand bids.

307. When both minors have been bid at the two- or three-level, 'double' by you shows at least four-card support for both unbid majors *or* four-card support for one major along with primary support for partner's suit. Reread this one.

LHO	Partner	RHO	You
	1♣	2◇	?

a) ♠A Q 7 6 ♡K 10 4 3 ◇4 3 ♣7 6 5
b) ♠J 9 8 7 ♡4 3 ◇4 3 ♣A K 10 6 5
c) ♠K J 4 3 ♡Q 3 ◇8 7 6 5 ♣Q 3 2

With (a), double. Perfect.

With (b), double. If partner bids hearts, return to clubs.

With (c), pass. If you double and partner bids 2♡, you have painted yourself into a corner. A return to three clubs shows four-card club support, minimum.

308. When both majors have been bid, 'double' promises at least four cards in each of the unbid minors.

a)

LHO	Partner	RHO	You
	1♡	1♠	dbl

b)

LHO	Partner	RHO	You
	1♡	2♠	dbl

In both auctions the double strongly suggests at least four cards in each minor. However, in either sequence you could have six diamonds and a hand not strong enough to bid 2◇ or 3◇ directly. A 2◇ bid shows 10+ HCP and a 3◇ bid shows 12+ HCP, normally played as a game force.

309. The lower the level of the negative double, the more precise the requirements. Many negative doubles made at the three- and four-levels simply say, 'I have a good hand with no long suit and no great support for your suit, but I think it is our hand. Do the right thing!'

LHO	Partner	RHO	You
	1♡	3♠	?

♠7 6 5 ♡5 4 ◇A K 8 7 ♣A J 8 7

Double — what else can you do? Even though you have no long suit, you can't pass and let them steal you blind. A negative double saves the day.

310. A negative double at the two-level, or a negative double of a 1♠ overcall with *four* hearts forcing partner to the two-level, shows a minimum of 8 HCP. A negative double at the three-level shows a minimum of 10 HCP.

311. When counting points, do not include jacks and queens in the opponent's suit — unless you intend to bid notrump, or are a masochist.

312. A big problem is how to handle a five-card major that must be shown at the two-level. If the suit is strong, bid the suit with 10+ HCP and double with 7-9 HCP. If the suit is weak, double with 7-10 HCP.

LHO	Partner	RHO	You
	1◇	1♠	?

a) ♠65 ♡AKJ87 ◇Q54 ♣1087
b) ♠754 ♡J6432 ◇Q2 ♣AQJ

With (a), bid 2♡. You are just barely strong enough; the ◇Q carries extra weight.

With (b), double and hope to bid hearts at the two-level, denying the strength for a direct 2♡ response.

313. In competition, strong six-card major suits can be shown at the two-level with as few as 9 HCP.

LHO	Partner	RHO	You
	1♣	1♠	?

a) ♠K4 ♡AQ10432 ◇87 ♣987
b) ♠87 ♡Q87654 ◇K4 ♣Q87

With (a), bid 2♡. Your ♠K is very likely worth a full trick.

With (b), double and hope to bid 2♡ next, even though partner will play you for a five-card suit, it's the best you can do with this hand.

314. A negative double followed by a new suit is not forcing. In order to create a force after making a negative double, you have to cuebid.

LHO	Partner	RHO	You
	1♣	2◇	dbl
pass	3♣	pass	?

♠ A K J 4 ♡ K Q 10 4 ◇ 8 7 ♣ 8 7 6

Bid 3◇ to create a force. If you bid a major, you are showing a five-card suit and 7-9/10 HCP. Not exactly what you have.

315. A negative double followed by a raise of partner's second suit is not forcing.

LHO	Partner	RHO	You
	1♣	1♠	dbl
pass	2♡	pass	?

a) ♠ A 4 ♡ A J 7 6 ◇ Q 10 4 3 ♣ 8 7 6
b) ♠ A 4 ♡ A J 7 6 ◇ K J 10 4 ♣ 8 7 6

With (a), raise to 3♡, invitational.
   With (b), raise to 4♡. The one who knows, goes.

316. A negative double followed by a 2NT rebid shows 10-12 HCP and is not forcing.

LHO	Partner	RHO	You
	1♣	1♠	dbl
2♠	pass	pass	?

a) ♠ A J 4 ♡ Q 10 8 7 ◇ A 9 ♣ 9 7 3 2
b) ♠ A J 4 ♡ Q J 8 7 ◇ A Q ♣ 5 4 3 2

With (a), bid 2NT, invitational.
   With (b), bid 3NT. The one who knows, goes.

317. If, after you make a negative double, your left-hand opponent raises, and the bidding comes back dead to you, a repeat double by you is also for takeout, showing extra strength.

LHO	Partner	RHO	You
	1♣	1♡	dbl
2♡	pass	pass	?

♠ A Q 9 6   ♡ 6 5 4   ◇ K J 9 3   ♣ 10 4

Double again to show 10+ HCP.

318. When most of your strength is in the opponent's suit, avoid a negative double. It is very misleading. Either pass or bid notrump. Reread this one.

LHO	Partner	RHO	You
	1◇	1♡	?

a)   ♠ 10 8 7 6   ♡ A Q 10 4   ◇ J 4   ♣ J 10 3
b)   ♠ 10 8 7 6   ♡ K Q J 4   ◇ 8 7   ♣ 9 8 3

With (a), respond 1NT, showing 8-10 HCP.

With (b), pass. It would be a blunder to double with this hand to show four spades. It would also be a blunder to respond 1NT. You are not strong enough. Patience is a great virtue.

319. If you pass a one-level overcall and partner reopens with a takeout double, a 1NT response shows 5-7 HCP. It is weaker than a direct response of 1NT. See (b) in previous tip. If partner reopens with a double in that example, you have a choice between bidding 1NT or 1♠.

*320. When you play negative doubles, you cannot make an immediate penalty double. With a strong five- or six-card holding in the opponent's suit, don't gasp, just pass. It is mega-important to pass ethically so partner is not aware of your great strength.

LHO	Partner	RHO	You
	1◇	1♡	?

a)   ♠ 7 4 2   ♡ A Q 10 8 6   ◇ 3   ♣ Q 9 8 7
b)   ♠ 6 4 3 2   ♡ K Q 9 7 3 2   ◇ 3   ♣ A 8

On both hands, pass. If partner reopens with a double, pass again.

*321. Assume partner opens, your right-hand opponent overcalls, you pass, and your left-hand opponent bids a new suit passed back to you. If you bid your right-hand opponent's suit, that bid is natural and not forcing.

LHO	Partner	RHO	You
	1◇	1♡	pass
2♣	pass	pass	?

♠ 9 8 4   ♡ K Q 10 9 6 4   ◇ Q 7   ♣ J 9

Bid 2♡.

322. A delayed double after both opponents bid is a penalty double of right-hand opponent's suit! It also shows 10+ HCP with some outside strength.

LHO	Partner	RHO	You
	1◇	1♡	pass
2♣	pass	pass	?

♠ J 7 6   ♡ A Q 10 5 4   ◇ A 4   ♣ 8 7 6

Double, telling partner (1) that you have hearts; (2) that your side has more HCP than their side; (3) to do something intelligent.

*323. A delayed double after left-hand opponent raises is a penalty double.

LHO	Partner	RHO	You
	1♡	2◇	pass
3◇	pass	pass	?

♠ 9 7 5   ♡ 6 5   ◇ A J 10 4   ♣ K 8 7 6

Double — this one says that you have diamonds. Finally! Not so fast! Some like to play that 'double' in this sequence shows a weak freak with five spades and five or six clubs, for example:

♠ J 10 7 3 2   ♡ 4   ◇ 6   ♣ K 10 7 5 4 2

Take your pick. Neither one comes up very often! However, it helps if both you and partner are on the same wavelength.

324. A negative double with three cards in partner's major is rare. Do not even consider doing it with less than 11 HCP. Even then, you must jump to confirm the support. Partner is not expecting three-card major-suit support when you make a negative double.

LHO	Partner	RHO	You
	1♠	2♡	?

♠ A J 4   ♡ 8 7 6 5   ◇ K Q 4   ♣ Q J 3

Double and then jump to 4♠ to describe this awkward hand. (A direct cuebid of 3♡ is supposed to show primary — four-card — trump support.)

REBIDDING AS OPENER AFTER RESPONDER MAKES A NEGATIVE DOUBLE

325. In a nutshell, with a minimum hand, make a minimum rebid. With an invitational hand, make a jump rebid; with a game-going hand, bid game or cuebid.

*326. After partner doubles a 1♡ overcall, rebid as if partner had responded 1♠ on a four-card suit with at least 6 HCP — although he could have much more. If he does, you'll hear about it.

LHO	Partner	RHO	You
			1♣
1♡	dbl	pass	?

a)   ♠A 4 3 2   ♡K 7 4   ◇3 2   ♣A J 9 8
b)   ♠A 4 3 2   ♡7 4   ◇3 2   ♣A K Q 3 2
c)   ♠A Q 8 4   ♡7 4   ◇K 4   ♣A K 7 3 2
d)   ♠A Q 8 4   ♡7 4   ◇A 4   ♣A K 7 3 2
e)   ♠7 4   ♡A Q 4   ◇J 4 3   ♣A J 9 8 7
f)   ♠7 4 3   ♡A Q 4   ◇K 4 3   ♣A K Q 4
g)   ♠7   ♡A 5 4   ◇A K J 4   ♣K Q 7 6 5
h)   ♠7 4   ♡Q 5   ◇Q 7 6 5   ♣A K Q 7 6
i)   ♠K Q 5 4   ♡A 7 6   ◇2   ♣A K 9 8 7

With (a), bid 1♠, the weakest spade bid possible, showing 12-14 support points.

    With (b), bid 2♠, showing 15-16 support points.

    With (c), bid 3♠, showing 17-18 support points.

    With (d), bid 4♠, showing 19-20 support points.

    With (e), bid 1NT.

With (f), bid 2NT.

With (g), bid 2◇, a forcing reverse showing 17+ HCP.

With (h), bid 2♣ — the same bid you would have made over a 1♠ response.

With (i), bid 3◇, a splinter — the same bid you would have made over a 1♠ response.

It seems a very simple and logical approach: pretend partner responded 1♠ with a four-card suit, and make your normal rebid.

*327. After partner doubles a 1♠ overcall, rebid as if partner had responded 1♡ on a four-card suit with 8+ HCP. When you force your partner to bid at the two-level you should have 8+ HCP to make a negative double.

LHO	Partner	RHO	You
			1◇
1♠	dbl	pass	?

a) ♠KJ4 ♡43 ◇KQ765 ♣A104
b) ♠KJ4 ♡43 ◇AK765 ♣AK4
c) ♠53 ♡10432 ◇AK74 ♣AJ4
d) ♠53 ♡AK74 ◇AK876 ♣98
e) ♠A4 ♡AQ87 ◇AK876 ♣J9
f) ♠4 ♡54 ◇AK876 ♣AQ987
g) ♠4 ♡54 ◇AKQ87 ♣AKQ108

With (a), bid 1NT.

With (b), bid 2NT.

With (c), bid 2♡.

With (d), bid 3♡.

With (e), bid 4♡.

With (f), bid 2♣ — partner has not promised clubs, just four hearts.

With (g), bid 3♣ — a game force. Some play a jump shift is invitational in this sequence.

328. After partner doubles 1◇, showing at least four cards in each major (possibly five hearts and four spades), jump rebids in the majors are invitational.

LHO	Partner	RHO	You
			1♣
1◇	dbl	pass	?

a) ♠A 10 4 2   ♡4 3   ◇7 6 5   ♣A K J 4
b) ♠A Q 4 2   ♡4   ◇8 6 5   ♣A K 4 3 2
c) ♠A Q 10 4   ♡Q 4   ◇3 2   ♣A K J 8 4
d) ♠9 4   ♡A K Q 4   ◇3 2   ♣A K J 9 4

With (a), bid 1♠, showing 12-14 support points.

With (b), bid 2♠, showing 15-16 support points.

With (c), bid 3♠, showing 17-18 support points.

With (d), bid 4♡, showing 19-20 support points. When supporting partner's known four-card suit, give yourself 1 extra point for each doubleton plus 1 extra for having all of your points in your two longest suits — I call this a 'purity' point. This brings your total to 20 support points.

329. After partner doubles a two-level overcall, a 2NT rebid shows 14-16 HCP and 3NT shows 17-19. Non-jump bids show minimums; jumps are invitational; the cuebid is a game force.

LHO	Partner	RHO	You
			1♠
2◇	dbl	pass	?

a) ♠A J 9 3 2   ♡3 2   ◇K 4 3   ♣A 5 4
b) ♠A J 10 4 3   ♡3 2   ◇A Q 5   ♣K 3 2
c) ♠A 9 7 6 2   ♡A Q 9   ◇Q 4 3   ♣10 8
d) ♠A K 8 7 6   ♡A Q 7 6   ◇4 3   ♣9 8
e) ♠A K 8 7 6   ♡A Q 4 3   ◇4 3   ♣A 2
f) ♠A K J 10 8 7 6   ♡2   ◇4   ♣K Q 7 6
g) ♠A Q J 9 8 7   ♡2   ◇A 4 3   ♣K J 8
h) ♠A K 8 7 5   ♡A 10 3   ◇2   ♣A K 10 4
i) ♠A K 8 7 6   ♡A J 4 3   ◇2   ♣A 10 6
J) ♠A K 8 7 6   ♡3 2   ◇A K 4   ♣Q J 9

With (a), bid 2♠ — not strong enough to rebid 2NT.

With (b), bid 2NT. Perfect.

*With (c), bid 2♡! You are not strong enough to bid 2NT, and though dangerous it is safer to bid 2♡, a suit partner must have, rather than 2♠, a suit partner doesn't have. Just pray he doesn't raise! (See Tip 324.)

With (d), bid 3♡, invitational.

With (e), bid 4♡. You are too strong to invite.

With (f), bid 4♠. You are too strong to invite with 3♠.

With (g), bid 3♠, invitational.

With (h), bid 3◇, a game force. You are looking for more information.

With (i), bid 4◇, a splinter raise of hearts, the suit partner has promised.

With (j), bid 3NT.

330. Do not pass a one- or two-level negative double unless you have both length (at least five cards) and intermediates in the opponent's suit. (Atypically you might pass holding four cards, all top honors.)

LHO	Partner	RHO	You
			1♡
2♣	dbl	pass	?

a) ♠A 4 ♡K Q 10 4 3 ◇3 ♣K Q 10 9 7
b) ♠A 4 ♡K Q 10 5 4 ◇6 5 ♣A Q 7 6
c) ♠A 4 ♡K J 8 7 6 ◇A 10 9 6 ♣10 8
d) ♠A 4 3 ♡K 10 8 6 2 ◇10 ♣K Q J 9

With (a), pass. You should only be so lucky.

With (b), bid 2NT. Your clubs are not strong enough to pass.

With (c), bid 3◇, a bid that should hit you in the face.

With (d), pass. Your best chance for a plus. With partner having spades and diamonds, where are they going to get eight tricks?

331. The higher the level of the negative double, the less strength you need in the opponent's suit to pass. With a balanced hand and three cards in the opponent's suit, a pass becomes a viable option.

LHO	Partner	RHO	You
			1♠
3◇	dbl	pass	?

a) ♠ A K 8 7 6 ♡ 5 4 ◇ A 3 2 ♣ K 10 8
b) ♠ A K 8 7 6 ♡ Q J 5 ◇ 3 2 ♣ K 8 7

With (a), pass. Partner is presumed short in spades, making your hand attractive defensively.

*With (b), this one is a little scary. There is no clear-cut action. Why I include hands that I'm not sure what to bid with is beyond me. I'm a passenger. The ♣K figures to be in dummy, he said wishfully. The possibilities are pass, 3♡ or 3♠. Be my guest.

332. Big tip coming up: Assume you open the bidding, your left-hand opponent overcalls, and there are two passes back to you. If you are short in the opponent's suit (void, singleton or small doubleton), there is a good chance that partner might be lurking over there with a penalty double of the opponent's suit. Ask yourself the following question: If partner had made a penalty double of this overcall, would you have passed? If the answer is yes, reopen the bidding with a takeout double; if the answer is no, bid something else.

LHO	Partner	RHO	You
			1◇
1♡	pass	pass	?

a) ♠ A 8 7 6 ♡ 3 ◇ Q J 8 7 ♣ K Q 5 4
b) ♠ K Q 4 ♡ 5 4 ◇ A J 3 2 ♣ K 7 6 3
c) ♠ 2 ♡ 9 ◇ A Q 10 8 7 6 ♣ K Q 9 8 7

With (a), double. If partner had made a penalty double of 1♡, you would have passed — I hope.

With (b), double — same reason.

With (c), bid 2♣. You would not have passed a penalty double of 1♡.

333. Assume you open the bidding, your left-hand opponent overcalls, there are two passes back to you, and you have length in their suit (three or more cards, exceptionally, a strong doubleton). Now it is safe to assume that partner does *not* have a penalty double of their suit.

Therefore, partner figures to be weak. In order to reopen the bidding with length in the opponent's suit, you need extra values, either high cards or distributional.

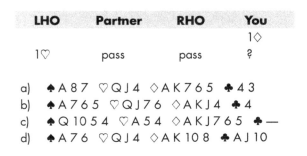

LHO	Partner	RHO	You
			1◇
1♡	pass	pass	?

a) ♠A 8 7 ♡Q J 4 ◇A K 7 6 5 ♣4 3
b) ♠A 7 6 5 ♡Q J 7 6 ◇A K J 4 ♣4
c) ♠Q 10 5 4 ♡A 5 4 ◇A K J 7 6 5 ♣—
d) ♠A 7 6 ♡Q J 4 ◇A K 10 8 ♣A J 10

With (a), pass. Nothing plus nothing equals nothing.

With (b), pass. Partner couldn't make a negative double or support diamonds. Where are you going?

With (c), bid 1♠. You can't give up on this hand.

With (d), bid 1NT. A reopening bid of 1NT shows 18-19 HCP.

WHEN YOU DOUBLE AN ARTIFICIAL BID; WHEN YOU DOUBLE 3NT

334. The main reason to double an artificial bid is to invite the lead of that suit.

335. A double of an artificial bid is a penalty double.

336. A double of any low-level artificial bid (think of a Stayman 2♣ response) requires a strong holding in the suit — either five cards headed by three of the top five honors, or six cards headed by two of the top four honors. Bidding the artificial suit, typically at the three-level, shows the equivalent of a vulnerable opening three-bid.

LHO	Partner	RHO	You
1NT	pass	2♣	?

a)   ♠43   ♡A76   ◇84   ♣KJ10632
b)   ♠43   ♡AK6   ◇84   ♣J87654
c)   ♠4   ♡54   ◇K109   ♣KQJ10543

With (a), double. You have the length and the strength.
    With (b), pass. You have the length, but not the strength.
    With (c), overcall 3♣ to show a vulnerable opening 3♣ bid.

337. The double of a four-level (or higher) artificial bid requires strength, not length. A three-card holding headed by two of the top three honors or even the king in back of a presumed ace is enough.

LHO	Partner	RHO	You
1♠	pass	3♠	pass
4◇	pass	4♡	?

a) ♠ 4 3 ♡ K Q 10 ◇ 8 7 6 5 ♣ 10 8 7 6
b) ♠ 4 3 ♡ Q 9 8 7 6 5 ◇ 7 2 ♣ K Q 9

With (a), double. You want a heart lead against a spade contract. You should also double with ♡KJx.

With (b), pass. You do not want to encourage a heart lead; you prefer a club lead.

338. Do not double an artificial bid if you are likely to be on lead unless you suffer from amnesia and need a reminder of what to lead.

LHO	Partner	RHO	You
		1♠	pass
3♠	pass	4♣	pass
4◇	pass	4♡	?

♠ 4 3 ♡ K Q J 8 ◇ 8 7 6 ♣ 10 7 4 2

Pass. Do not double for a heart lead. You will be on lead!

339. To double an artificial bid when you will be on lead hurts your own cause. Not only do you warn your opponents of your strength, you also give the next hand options not previously available such as pass and redouble.

340. The common artificial bids to be on the lookout for (when partner will be on lead) are:

i) Stayman 2♣ and 3♣ responses to 1NT and 2NT opening bids;
ii) Transfer responses to 1NT and 2NT opening bids;
iii) Cuebids;
iv) Blackwood or Gerber responses;
v) Splinter bids;
vi) Drury;
vii) The fourth suit, particularly at the three-level, usually an artificial bid asking partner for a stopper in that suit.

341. When you fail to double a Blackwood response, you warn partner that you have no great interest in that suit being led.

LHO	Partner	RHO	You
1♠	pass	3♠	pass
4NT	pass	5♣	?

♠ 8 7   ♡ J 7 6 5   ◇ 10 8 7 5   ♣ K Q J

Don't just sit there! Seize the opportunity to double. This ensures a club lead against an eventual spade contract. Passing 5♣ is a bridge blunder!

342. After you double a low-level artificial bid and later bid a new suit, you show a two-suited hand.

LHO	Partner	RHO	You
1NT	pass	2♡	dbl
2♠	pass	pass	3♣

♠ 4   ♡ A J 10 5 4   ◇ 3 2   ♣ K Q J 9 8

The double shows long hearts, and the club bid shows long clubs. *Voilà*, you have shown your hand. What a player!

343. Partner's double of 3NT asks for a particular lead. It doesn't hurt to know the rules.

344. If no suits have been bid, partner's double of 3NT announces the possession of some solid suit, usually a major.

LHO	Partner	RHO	You
		1NT	pass
3NT	dbl	all pass	

♠ Q 7 6 5   ♡ 7 6   ◇ Q 5 4 3 2   ♣ 8 7

Partner has a solid suit. It can't be spades or diamonds, so it must be hearts or clubs. With a blind choice between a major and a minor, lead the major.

345. When neither you nor your partner has bid, lead dummy's first bid suit.

LHO	Partner	RHO	You
		1♡	pass
1♠	pass	1NT	pass
2NT	pass	3NT	pass
pass	dbl	all pass	

♠ 8 4   ♡ Q 8 7 5   ◇ Q J 9 3 2   ♣ 10 5

Don't try to be a genius. Lead the ♠8, as partner requested.

346. If you have *not* bid and partner has overcalled at the two- or three-level, lead partner's suit.

LHO	Partner	RHO	You
		1♠	pass
2◇	2♡	2NT	pass
3NT	dbl	all pass	

♠ J 10 8 7   ♡ 4   ◇ 9 6   ♣ Q J 10 5 4 3

Lead your singleton heart. The lead of the ♣Q is the equivalent to a slap in partner's face.

*347. If *you* overcall at the one-level and partner passes throughout and later doubles 3NT:

  i) If partner had a chance to support your one-level overcalled suit at the *two*-level and did not, lead dummy's first bid suit.
  ii) If partner had no chance to support your suit at the two-level, lead your suit.

LHO	Partner	RHO	You
		1♣	1♡
1♠	pass	1NT	pass
2NT	pass	3NT	pass
pass	dbl	all pass	

♠ 8 4   ♡ K J 8 6 4   ◊ A J 10   ♣ 5 4 3

Partner had a chance to support you at the two-level and did not. Lead the ♣8.

LHO	Partner	RHO	You
		1♣	1♡
3♣	pass	3NT	pass
pass	dbl	all pass	

♠ 8 4   ♡ K J 8 6 4   ◊ A J 10   ♣ 5 4 3

Partner had no chance to support your suit at the two-level. Lead the ♡6.

*348. If you open 1♡ or 1♠ and later double 3NT without having had a chance bid a secondary suit at the two-level, your double asks for a lower-ranking unbid suit. The expected lead is the major and you need the double to divert partner away from it.

LHO	Partner	RHO	You
			1♠
1NT	pass	2NT	pass
3NT	pass	pass	dbl
all pass			

♠ J 8 6 5 3   ♡ A 2   ◊ 4 3   ♣ A K Q 10

Go for it! Double to forbid a spade lead. Partner knows you have a very strong side suit and can usually tell from his or her hand which it is. If partner can't tell, find one who can.

*349. After partner opens 1♣ or 1◊ and later doubles 3NT, the converse is true. There is a strong inclination to assume partner's minor-suit opening is either short or weak after the opponents arrive in notrump. The double reassures you that it is not. Lead partner's minor suit!

LHO	Partner	RHO	You
	1♣	dbl	pass
2♡	pass	2NT	pass
3NT	dbl	all pass	

♠ J 10 9 4   ♡ J 7 6 5   ◇ 8 4 3 2   ♣ 2

Lead a club, any club.

*350. If everybody bids a suit, consider suicide, but then lead dummy's first bid suit if it was bid at the one-level. If partner wants his own suit led, the expected lead, he should pass. If dummy's first bid suit was bid at the two-level, lead partner's suit.

LHO	Partner	RHO	You
		1♣	1♡
1♠	2◇	2NT	pass
3NT	dbl	all pass	

Partner wants a spade lead. If he had wanted a diamond lead, that's life.

351. The double of a *voluntarily* bid suit slam, as opposed to a sacrifice, is similar to a double of 3NT; it asks for an unusual lead. If partner thinks the normal lead will defeat the slam, partner does not double.

352. There are certain leads that can be eliminated when partner doubles a voluntarily bid suit slam:

  i) A trump
  ii) Any suit partner has bid
  iii) The unbid suit — if partner has not bid.

353. The most common reason to double a slam is having a void, particularly if the doubler has preempted.

LHO	Partner	RHO	You
	4♡	4♠	pass
4NT	pass	5♡	pass
6♠	dbl	all pass	

♠ 9 4   ♡ 3 2   ◇ 10 8 7 6 5 4   ♣ Q J 10

Partner probably has a diamond void with a side ace. A heart lead is out. Lead a diamond. Don't tell me you wanted to lead the ♣Q.

354. When a void seems remote, another possibility is that partner has an AK or AQ, usually in dummy's first bid suit. It is important to work out which is more likely, because if you don't, you will never hear the end of it!

355. A true sadist is someone who doubles a suit slam with the AK of trumps and then enjoys watching partner squirm trying to work out the 'killing' lead.

356. Trying to figure out which suit to lead against a doubled suit slam is somewhat akin to trying to figure out who the killer is in a movie mystery. In the movies, it's the butler; at the bridge table, it's usually the last suit you would have thought of leading.

357. The double of a *notrump* slam asks for the lead of dummy's first bid suit. Much easier to deal with as giving partner a ruff is no longer a consideration.

CUEBIDS, CUEBIDS

Cuebids come in all shapes and sizes. They can:

  i) Show a control for slam purposes;
  ii) Show a two-suited hand;
  iii) Show a strong raise;
  iv) Create a force;
  v) Ask for a stopper;
  vi) Show a stopper.

358. After major-suit agreement at the three-level or higher, or after minor-suit agreement at the four-level or higher, new suits are slam-oriented cuebids.

a)

Opener	Responder
1◊	1♡
3♡	4♣

b)

Opener	Responder
1♣	1◊
3◊	3♡

In (a), 4♣ is a cuebid because there has been major-suit agreement at the three-level.

In (b), 3♡ is not considered a control-showing cuebid because it is beneath the level of 3NT. More often than not it shows a heart stopper in the hope that partner can bid 3NT with a spade stopper.

359. After minor-suit agreement at the two- or three-level, new suits are considered efforts to get to 3NT — unless the subsequent bidding proves differently.

Opener	Responder
1♣	3♣
3◊	3NT
4♡	?

The 3◊ bid is considered a stopper-showing bid in an effort to get to 3NT. However, when responder bids 3NT and opener removes to 4♡, 4♡ is a slam try and 3◊ should be considered one as well.

360. A cuebid in response to a major-suit opening bid by an unpassed hand guarantees primary support and shows a limit raise or stronger. This presumes that a direct jump to the three-level of partner's suit in competition is preemptive.

LHO	Partner	RHO	You
	1♠	2♡	?

♠ A K 8 7   ♡ 3 2   ◇ K J 9 8   ♣ Q 9 8

Bid 3♡ to show primary spade support with limit raise values or better. This assumes you are playing that a jump to 3♠ in competition is preemptive (3 to 6 HCP). If you play limit raises in competition, a cuebid of 3♡ is a game force.

*361. A cuebid in response to a minor-suit opening bid guarantees primary support with limit raise values or better. This presumes that a jump to the three-level of partner's minor in competition is preemptive.

LHO	Partner	RHO	You
	1♣	1♡	?

♠ A 7 6   ♡ 7 6   ◇ K J 8   ♣ K J 10 7 6

Playing limit raises, this hand is too strong to bid 3♣. Bid 2♡, and see what happens. A good partner will turn up with a heart stopper. If you play forcing jump raises, respond 3♣.

To summarize: If you play preemptive jump raises in competition, a cuebid is a limit raise or better. If you play limit raises in competition, a cuebid is a game force.

362. A cuebid followed by a new suit is 100% forcing. No, make that 1000%.

LHO	Partner	RHO	You
1♡	dbl	2♡	3♡
pass	3♠	pass	4◇

♠ A   ♡ 6 5   ◇ A 10 9 8 7 6   ♣ K Q 10 5

The 4◇ bid, preceded by a cuebid, is forcing. There could even be a slam here.

363. Jump cuebids show shortness plus primary support. Jump cuebids are game forcing and slam invitational.

LHO	Partner	RHO	You
	1♡	2♣	?

♠ A 7 6   ♡ Q J 8 7 6   ◇ A 8 7 6   ♣ 3

Bid 4♣, a splinter jump, impressing the whole table with your mastery of the latest gadgets.

364. A direct jump cuebid in a *major* suit before partner has bid asks partner to bid notrump with a stopper in the opponent's suit.

LHO	Partner	RHO	You
		1♠	?

♠ 4   ♡ A 9   ◇ Q 10 4   ♣ A K Q J 8 7 6

Bid 3♠, asking for a spade stopper. If partner doesn't have one, you will play the hand in clubs. If the opening bid is 1♣ or 1◇, a direct jump to the three-level in opener's minor suit is natural and preemptive. Think of it as an opening three-bid in that suit.

365. After you, partner, and one opponent have bid and there has been no major-suit agreement, a bid in the opponent's suit asks partner to bid notrump with a stopper in that suit.

LHO	Partner	RHO	You
			1♣
1◇	3♣¹	pass	?

1. Limit raise.

♠ A J 4   ♡ A 10 9   ◇ 3 2   ♣ K Q 10 8 7

You would like to play 3NT if partner has a diamond stopper. Bid 3◇ to ask: a good partner will have one. If you play 3♣ is weak in competition, pass. Quickly.

366. If the opponents have bid *two* suits (as opposed to one), a bid in one of their suits *shows* a stopper and asks partner to bid notrump with the other suit stopped.

LHO	Partner	RHO	You
			1♣
1♠	2♣	2◇	?

♠A 10 8   ♡A 5   ◇8 7   ♣A K J 8 7 6

Bid 2♠ to show a spade stopper, asking partner to bid notrump with a diamond stopper.

367. The Bottom Line: After minor-suit agreement, the opponents having bid *one* suit, bidding that suit *asks* for a stopper in that suit. When the opponents have bid *two* suits, a cuebid in one suit *shows* a stopper in that suit and asks partner to bid notrump with a stopper in the other suit.

368. A cuebid at opener's first opportunity after partner has bid a new suit is ambiguous. Opener can have one of two things in mind:

    i) Opener may have a fit for responder's suit.
    ii) Opener may wish to ask for a stopper, holding a solid suit.

LHO	Partner	RHO	You
			1♣
1♠	2♡	pass	?

♠A 2   ♡A K 9 4   ◇7 6   ♣A K 10 9 8

Bid 2♠. When you later support hearts, your cuebid will be interpreted as a slam try.

LHO	Partner	RHO	You
			1♣
1♠	2♡	pass	?

♠432   ♡4   ◇AK   ♣AKQ8765

Bid 2♠! This time you are asking for a spade stopper. How will partner know? Partner will have to be patient. With a spade stopper, partner's *first obligation* is to bid notrump. If you later remove to hearts (see previous example), partner will know that your cuebid was based on a heart fit rather than a solid minor suit. As long as each of you knows the two possibilities, nothing too terrible can happen. (Send no letters.)

EVALUATING YOUR HAND

369. Do not be a slave to your point count. There are other, sometimes more important, factors to be considered.

370. Downgrade jacks and queens in suits bid by the opponents, unless partner makes a natural notrump bid.

LHO	Partner	RHO	You
	1♠	2◇	?

♠K J 4   ♡Q J 8 7   ◇6 5 4   ♣10 4 3

Raise to 2♠. Your heart strength could be worth something.

LHO	Partner	RHO	You
	1♠	2♡	?

♠K J 4   ♡Q J 8 7   ◇6 5 4   ♣10 4 3

Pass. You have too much potentially wasted secondary heart strength.

371. Avoid making any encouraging sounds with too much strength in the opponents' suit. Partner invariably thinks you have strength outside and bids too much. (See second example in the previous tip.)

372. Downgrade honor cards in suits that have been bid to your *left*, upgrade honor cards in suits that have been bid to your *right*, particularly kings and aces with yet another card. AQx, AJx, KQx, KJx. Those combinations are usually worth two tricks.

LHO	Partner	RHO	You
			1♠
2♡	2♠	pass	pass
3◇	pass	pass	?

♠ K J 8 7 6   ♡ A Q 4   ◇ K J 4   ♣ 3 2

Pass! Quickly! Your hand lost some of its value when LHO bid hearts. What little was left went down the drain when LHO bid diamonds.

373. Downgrade hands that have length in suits bid by the opponents, particularly your left-hand opponent.

LHO	Partner	RHO	You
			1♠
2♡	2♠	pass	?

♠ A Q 8 7 6   ♡ A J 7 6 5   ◇ K 3   ♣ 3

Pass. What are you going to do with those hearts? If LHO had passed, you would have enough to bid on, but you have been forewarned! Even if partner is short in hearts, RHO, also short in hearts, will be poised to overtrump dummy.

374. For notrump evaluation, downgrade balanced hands lacking intermediate spot cards, nines and tens. On the other hand, upgrade balanced hands with excellent intermediate spot cards in conjunction with other honor cards, particularly in four-card suits (for example, A109x).

    a) ♠ K 4 3   ♡ A 2   ◇ J 5 4 3   ♣ J 8 7 6
    b) ♠ K 10 2   ♡ A 2   ◇ J 10 5 4   ♣ J 9 8 7

Hand (a) counts out to 9 points; (b) is worth *at least* 10.

375. Add 1 point to any hand that has all of its strength in the two long suits, a 'purity' point.

    a) ♠ K 8 7 6 5   ♡ Q 2   ◇ K J 10 4   ♣ Q 5
    b) ♠ A K 8 7 6   ♡ 4 2   ◇ K J 10 4   ♣ 3 2

Hand (b) is at least 1 point stronger than hand (a).

376. When considering a notrump bid, add 1 point for a five-card suit headed by three of the top five honors.

    a)   ♠ K 4 ♡ A J 10 ◇ K 6 5 ♣ Q J 10 7 6
    b)   ♠ K 4 ♡ A J 4 ◇ K 6 5 ♣ A Q 10 7 6

With (a), bid as if you had 15 points; with (b), bid as if you had 18 points.

377. When faced with borderline decisions, let the strength of the intermediate cards in the long suit be the determining factor.

LHO	Partner	RHO	You
			1♠
pass	2◇	pass	?

    a)   ♠ A 8 6 5 4 3 ♡ K 7 4 ◇ K Q ♣ Q 3
    b)   ♠ A K J 10 8 7 ♡ A Q 10 ◇ 4 3 2 ♣ 2

With (a), bid a conservative 2♠.
   With (b), bid an aggressive 3♠.

378. An ace and king in one suit is better than an ace in one suit and a king in another. This tip holds true for any two honor cards.

    a)   ♠ A K 4 ♡ 6 5 4 ◇ 6 5 4 ♣ K Q 8 7
    b)   ♠ A 3 2 ♡ K 5 4 ◇ K 8 7 ♣ Q 7 6 5

Hand (a) is stronger than hand (b).

379. With 5-5 or 6-5 distribution, bid aggressively if your strength is concentrated in your long suits. Be careful if it is not.

    a)   ♠ A Q 10 5 4 3 ♡ K Q 9 5 4 ◇ 5 4 ♣ —
    b)   ♠ Q 9 7 6 5 4 ♡ Q 9 6 5 4 ◇ A K ♣ —

Hand (a) is light years stronger than hand (b).

380. When an opponent shows a two-suited hand, be leery of having secondary honor cards in one of those suits ruffed away.

LHO	Partner	RHO	You
			1♡
1♠	2♡	pass	pass
3♢	pass	pass	?

♠ K Q J   ♡ A J 9 8 7   ♢ 3 2   ♣ Q J 9

Be careful! RHO likes diamonds and probably has a singleton spade. If LHO starts with the ace and another spade, you may not take many (or any!) spade tricks. Your best bet is to pass.

381. When partner shows a two-suited hand, upgrade honor cards in partner's long suits and aces in partner's short suits. Downgrade secondary honor cards in partner's short suits.

LHO	Partner	RHO	You
	1♠	pass	2♢
pass	2♡	pass	2NT
pass	3♡	pass	?

a) ♠ Q 4   ♡ Q 10 4   ♢ A 8 7 6 5   ♣ A 10 9
b) ♠ 10 9   ♡ Q 4   ♢ K Q 10 8 7   ♣ K Q 9 8

Hand (a) is enormous on the bidding with honors in partner's long suits and aces in partner's short suit. Cuebid 4♣.

Hand (b) is worse; bid 3NT. Your minor-suit intermediates should come in very handy.

382. Long broken suits increase in value when: (i) partner supports your long suit; (ii) partner is known to hold a balanced hand.

LHO	Partner	RHO	You
	1NT	pass	?

♠ K 8 7 6 4 3   ♡ 7 6 2   ♢ Q J 6 4   ♣ —

Your hand is easier to evaluate because you know partner has at least two spades. Make an effort to get to 4♠ via a transfer sequence followed by a raise.

LHO	Partner	RHO	You
	1♣	pass	1♠
pass	3♣	pass	?

♠K87643　♡762　◇QJ64　♣—

You are in a quandary. If partner has a few spades, you have a chance for game. If partner has a singleton spade, your hand is not worth much. What should you do? I'm a passenger. I know, 'no guts, no glory', but not on this hand, not with these spades.

383. Think in terms of tricks, not points, when holding an independent suit (a suit that can play easily opposite a singleton).

LHO	Partner	RHO	You
			1♠
pass	1NT	pass	?

♠KQJ9874　♡AKJ　◇43　♣2

You have an independent suit. Count tricks! You have close to nine tricks in your own hand — leap to 4♠. Bidding 3♠ is way too conservative.

384. Be patient when evaluating hands with singletons or voids. If your shortness is in partner's length, your hand loses value. If you have support plus shortness, your hand increases in value. Patience.

♠A876　♡5　◇A1043　♣8765

What is this hand worth? The truth is you can't tell until you hear the bidding. If partner bids spades, your hand is worth 11 points in support of spades. If partner bids hearts, you have an 8-point hand — actually less with a singleton in partner's longest suit.

*385. After you receive support and have a known eight-card fit, use the *Rule of Seven* to determine just how much your hand has improved. What? You've never heard of the Rule of Seven? Of course you haven't; I made it up, but it works!

LHO	Partner	RHO	You
			1♠
pass	2♠	pass	?

a)   ♠AQ876 ♡KQ54 ◇A2 ♣54
b)   ♠AQ876 ♡KQ54 ◇A32 ♣5

After your suit has been raised and you are sure of an eight-card fit, but cannot be sure of a nine-card or longer fit, add the lengths of your two longest suits (9) and subtract 7 from the total (9 − 7 = 2). Additionally, if you have a side singleton, add 1 extra point, and 2 extra points for a side-suit void.

Hand (a) increases in value by 2 points (subtract 7 from 9), and is now worth 17 points.

Hand (b) increases by 3 extra points because it has a singleton as well, and is now worth 18 points.

Bid 3♡ with both hands. Partner might have four or five hearts with three spades.

*386. When you are assured of a nine-card trump fit or longer, use the *Rule of Six*.

LHO	Partner	RHO	You
			1♠
pass	2♠	pass	?

♠AQ8765 ♡K4 ◇A876 ♣3

This time your hand increases by 5 points! Subtract 6 from the length of your two longest suits (10 − 6 = 4) giving you 4 extra points. You also have a side singleton, giving you 1 more point. Your 13-point frog has blossomed into an 18-point prince! Bid 4♠.

COMPETITIVE AUCTIONS

387. When the bid to your right is strong, a jump by you is weak.

LHO	Partner	RHO	You
		1NT	3◇

1NT is strong, so 3◇ is weak.

388. When the bid to your right is weak, a jump by you is strong.

LHO	Partner	RHO	You
		3♡	4♠

3♡ is weak, so 4♠ is strong.

LHO	Partner	RHO	You
1◇	dbl		2♡

'Double' is strong, so 2♡ is weak.

389. Any time you are in a game-forcing auction and your right-hand opponent intervenes, a pass by you is forcing. If you are not in a game-forcing auction and your right-hand opponent intervenes, a pass by you is not forcing.

LHO	Partner	RHO	You
			1♣
pass	2NT	3♡	?

♠ A Q 7 6   ♡ 5 4   ◇ K 7 6   ♣ Q J 9 8

Pass. Assuming 2NT is a game force, your pass is forcing. Maybe partner will have a better idea of what to do than you, for once. If you don't play 2NT as forcing, a pass is here is not forcing.

390. Any time you are in a game-forcing auction and your right-hand opponent bids, a double by you is for penalty.

LHO	Partner	RHO	You
			1♠
2♡	3◇	4♡	?

♠ A K 7 6 5   ♡ K Q 5   ◇ 3   ♣ Q 9 8 7

Double. Even though a pass is forcing (see previous tip), your hand is more suited to defense.

391. A raise in competition does not promise more than a raise made without competition; it simply denies a courtesy raise.

LHO	Partner	RHO	You
			1♠
pass	2♠	pass	

LHO	Partner	RHO	You
			1♠
2♡	2♠	pass	

Partner does not necessarily show a stronger hand in the second auction.

392. Many competitive bids at high levels are made under pressure. As a result, you may not always have what partner expects, or vice versa.

LHO	Partner	RHO	You
	1◇	4♡	?

a)   ♠ K Q J 10 7 6 4   ♡ 3   ◇ Q J 5   ♣ 4 2
b)   ♠ K Q J 10 7   ♡ 3   ◇ Q J 5 4   ♣ J 10 8

With (a), respond 4♠.
   With (b), respond 4♠. (Get the idea?)

393. When there is little chance of getting doubled, bid close games vulnerable against not. Opponents tend to sacrifice so you might as well reap the profits.

394. Good players are loath to make low-level penalty doubles without trump tricks. This means you can take liberties in low-level competitive auctions with a strong suit.

395. After raising partner to the two-level, seldom take the push to the three-level with a balanced hand if the opponents compete. To take the push you need a side-suit singleton or undisclosed four-card trump support.

LHO	Partner	RHO	You
			1◇
pass	1♡	pass	2♡
pass	pass	2♠	?

a) ♠4 ♡AK4 ◇A8765 ♣Q1043
b) ♠76 ♡AK42 ◇AQ87 ♣432
c) ♠64 ♡AK4 ◇AQ87 ♣7654

With (a), bid 3♣. You have a side-suit singleton plus attractive distribution.

With (b), bid 3♡. Even if your raise promised four hearts (some raise with three) you have a maximum with all of your strength concentrated in two suits, a plus.

With (c), pass. No reason to bid 3♡. You have neither a side-suit singleton nor a fourth trump.

396. When there is competition to your right that robs you of your normal rebid, pass with a minimum. Partner still has a chance to bid.

LHO	Partner	RHO	You
			1♡
pass	1♠	2◇	?

♠87 ♡AK876 ◇87 ♣KQ87

Pass. If RHO had not bid, you would have rebid 2♣. However, you need extra strength to rebid 3♣, a new suit at the three-level. No need to rebid hearts, partner already knows about that suit.

397. When there is competition to your right that does not rob you of your normal rebid, make it!

LHO	Partner	RHO	You
			1♡
pass	1♠	2◇	?

♠ A Q 4   ♡ A K 8 7 6   ◇ 4 3   ♣ 4 3 2

You were going to raise to 2♠ before the 2◇ overcall, so raise to 2♠ after the overcall. However, if you play support doubles, double 2◇ to show three spades. Playing support doubles, a raise to 2♠ would show four spades.

398. Low-level penalty doubles of suit contracts, or low-level passes of partner's takeout doubles, are based on trump length and strength, not high-card points.

399. It is easier to play a contract of 1NT than it is to defend one.

400. Be aggressive in the early stages of the auction. Bidding has a way of getting out of hand. Waiting in the bushes is for hunters, not bridge players.

401. After partner opens and second hand overcalls 1NT, double with 9 or more HCP. You have them outgunned.

LHO	Partner	RHO	You
	1♡	1NT	?

♠ A J 9   ♡ 3 2   ◇ K J 9 7 6   ♣ 8 7 6

Double. Do not bid 2◇. (See next tip.)

402. After partner opens and second hand overcalls 1NT, bidding a new suit, jumping in a new suit, or jumping in partner's suit all show weak distributional hands. Your failure to double (or bid 2NT showing a monstrous two-suiter) warns partner you are bidding on distribution, not strength.

LHO	Partner	RHO	You
	1♡	1NT	?

a) ♠ 5 4   ♡ 5 4   ◇ Q J 10 7 6 4   ♣ K 5 4
b) ♠ 4   ♡ 5 4   ◇ K Q J 8 5 3 2   ♣ 8 7 5
c) ♠ 3   ♡ J 10 5 4   ◇ Q 10 4 3 2   ♣ 4 3 2

With (a), bid 2◇, not forcing.
   With (b), bid 3◇, preemptive.
   With (c), bid 3♡, preemptive.

403. Be familiar with the distinction between these two sequences:

LHO	Partner	RHO	You
			1◇
pass	1♡	1♠	1NT

Here, you show 13-14 with two likely spade stoppers.

LHO	Partner	RHO	You
			1◇
1♠	pass	pass	1NT

Here, you show 18-19 — a hand too strong to open 1NT.

404. There are 2NT rebids, and there are 2NT rebids.

LHO	Partner	RHO	You
			1♡
2♣	2♠	pass	2NT

Your partner's two-level response was in a higher-ranking suit than your suit
and you are forced to bid something. Therefore a 2NT rebid shows a minimum hand in the 12-14 point range. A 3◇ rebid would not necessarily show
extras.

LHO	Partner	RHO	You
			1◇
1♡	1♠	2♡	2NT

You *voluntarily* bid 2NT after partner's one-level response. You could have passed with a minimum. This 2NT shows 18-19 HCP — as if RHO had passed.

405. A biggie: After you have limited your hand and your right-hand opponent bids, unless you wish to make a penalty double, or have some unusual feature partner can't know about, it is almost always right to pass. Remember, you are limited so partner knows your hand better than you know partner's.

LHO	Partner	RHO	You
			1NT
pass	pass	2♡	?

♠ A J 4   ♡ K J 4   ♢ K Q 8 7   ♣ Q J 4

Pass. You have no surprises. Give partner a chance to do something intelligent. He may surprise you.

406. After either you or your partner has made a natural notrump bid, any double by your side is a penalty double. Of course, there are two major exceptions almost universally played:

LHO	Partner	RHO	You
			1NT
2♡	pass	pass	dbl

You have opened 1NT and your *left* hand opponent has overcalled at the two-level and the bidding has been passed back to you. A double in this sequence is considered a takeout double. It shows a small doubleton heart with a maximum 1NT opening bid. Had your *right*-hand opponent overcalled 2♡, double would be for penalty.

You might have:

♠ A 6 5 3   ♡ 4 3   ♢ A K J 5   ♣ A J 7

LHO	Partner	RHO	You
			1NT
3♣	dbl	pass	

You have opened 1NT and your left-hand opponent has overcalled at the three-level. A double in this sequence by partner is considered to be the equivalent of Stayman. It is not a penalty double *per se*, although you are free to pass.

Partner might have:

♠ A J 8 7   ♡ K J 8 7   ◇ 6 5 4   ♣ 5 4

407. After a two-level overcall, a 2NT response to an opening bid shows 10-12 HCP and is not forcing. With 13-16 HCP, respond 3NT. When deciding between these bids, an ace, king, or queen in partner's long suit is generally worth an extra 2 points. A small singleton in partner's suit and/or a lack of intermediate cards is a downgrade of 1 point each.

LHO	Partner	RHO	You
	1♠	2♡	?

a) ♠ A 10 ♡ K J 8 ◇ Q 9 8 7 ♣ J 9 4 3
b) ♠ A 10 ♡ K J 8 ◇ A J 10 6 ♣ J 9 4 3

With (a), bid 2NT.

With (b), bid 3NT. This hand has upgrades coming out the wazoo. The ♠A is fitting in nicely with partner's five-card suit and you have all those intermediates — not to mention that the opposing heart honors are well placed for you.

408. The 'death' distribution for competing in a major to the three-level after partner has given you a single raise is 5-3-3-2. Minimum hands with this distribution do better to defend rather than play at the three-level.

LHO	Partner	RHO	You
			1♠
pass	2♠	3♡	?

♠ A Q 6 3 2   ♡ 8 7   ◇ Q J 5   ♣ A 7 2

Pass. Do not bid 3♠. You have a minimum with the 'death' distribution. You have a better chance of defeating 3♡ with your defensive type hand than of making 3♠ with all those losers.

409. A delayed double by second hand, when responder is unlimited and the opponents have not found a fit, is a penalty double.

LHO	Partner	RHO	You
		1♡	pass
1♠	pass	1NT/2♡	?

♠ 4   ♡ A Q 10 8 6   ◇ K J 8   ♣ A 10 4 2

Double — penalties! Responder is unlimited and the opponents have *not* found a fit. Partner will expect you to have strong hearts with short spades.

410. A delayed double by second hand after the opponents have found a fit is for takeout.

LHO	Partner	RHO	You
		1♡	pass
1♠	pass	2♠	dbl

Your double is for takeout because they have found a fit. Think of a 1-4-4-4 pattern with a singleton spade and opening bid values.

*411. A delayed double after a 1NT response is for takeout if opener bids a new suit.

LHO	Partner	RHO	You
		1♡	pass
1NT	pass	2♣	dbl

♠ A J 8 7   ♡ K 4 3   ◇ K 10 7 4 2   ♣ 3

This time your double is for takeout because responder has bid 1NT and opener has made a non-forcing rebid in a new suit.

412. Once you push the opponents to the five-level, it is usually right to let them play there or double. After all, if they were happy to play at the four-level, how thrilled can they be to play at the five-level? It has often been said that the five-level belongs to the opponents.

413. In a competitive auction, do not make a premature penalty double with an undisclosed fit for partner. First, show the support, then, if the opponents persist, wield the axe.

Both vulnerable

LHO	Partner	RHO	You
1♡	3♠	4♡	?

♠ A 10 5   ♡ A 10 9 8   ◇ 4   ♣ Q 10 8 7 6

Don't double! Bid 4♠ and then double 5♡ if you get the chance.

WHEN AN OPENING BID IS PASSED AROUND TO YOU

414. In the protective seat, also called the balancing seat, also called the passout seat, you are allowed to bid with 2 to 3 points fewer than in the direct seat. Takeout doubles start as low as 9 HCP and simple overcalls at 7 HCP. The key is to be short in the opener's suit.

LHO	Partner	RHO	You
1♢	pass	pass	?

a) ♠ A 9 8 7 ♡ K 5 4 3 ♢ 4 ♣ Q 7 6 5
b) ♠ Q 10 8 7 6 ♡ A J 4 ♢ 4 3 ♣ 10 8 7

With (a), double.
    With (b), bid 1♠.
    In direct seat, you should pass the 1♢ opening bid with either hand.

415. If the opening bid is 1♣ or 1♢, reopen with 1NT holding 11-14 balanced. With 15-17, double and then bid 1NT.

LHO	Partner	RHO	You
1♣	pass	pass	?

a) ♠ A J 3 ♡ Q 10 4 ♢ Q 9 3 2 ♣ A 8 7
b) ♠ A K 3 ♡ K 10 4 ♢ Q 9 3 2 ♣ A 10 4

With (a), bid 1NT.
    With (b), double and then bid 1NT.

416. If the opening bid is 1♡ or 1♠, reopen with 1NT holding 11-15 balanced. With 16-18, double and then bid the cheapest number of notrump possible.

LHO	Partner	RHO	You
1♠	pass	pass	?

a) ♠KJ76 ♡1087 ◇AJ ♣KJ54
b) ♠KJ7 ♡A102 ◇AJ9 ♣KJ108

With (a), bid 1NT.
   With (b), double and then bid 2NT.

417. With a balanced hand and 19-20 HCP, bid 2NT immediately. With a balanced hand and 21-22 HCP, double and then jump in notrump.

LHO	Partner	RHO	You
1♣	pass	pass	?

a) ♠AK4 ♡K4 ◇AQ87 ♣A1052
b) ♠AK4 ♡K4 ◇AQ87 ♣AQ105

With (a), bid 2NT.
   With (b), double and then jump in notrump.

*418. There is no such animal as the Unusual Notrump in the balancing seat by an unpassed hand. A bid of 1NT shows 11-14/15 HCP, and 2NT shows 19-20. With in-between ranges, double and then bid notrump. If the opening bid is 1♡ or 1♠ and you have both minors, start with 2◇ and hope to be able to bid 3♣ next.

LHO	Partner	RHO	You
1♠	pass	pass	?

a) ♠AJ4 ♡A1075 ◇K1076 ♣108
b) ♠AJ42 ♡A10 ◇KQ86 ♣AQ3
c) ♠4 ♡65 ◇AJ1054 ♣KQ1086

With (a), bid 1NT
   With (b), bid 2NT.

With (c), bid 2◊; 2NT shows 19-20 balanced. If you were a passed hand, you could bid 2NT, 'unusual', at this point.

419. Reopening the bidding with a cuebid shows a two-suited hand with at least five cards in each suit. Over 1♣ or 1◊ a cuebid shows the majors.

After 1♡ or 1♠ a cuebid of 2♡ or 2♠ shows five cards in the other major with five or six cards in an unknown minor. Partner bids 2NT to ask for the minor. The range of most two-suited cuebids is 7-11 or 15+ HCP. With 12-14 HCP, called the 'tweeners', start by bidding the higher-ranking suit and hope you can get the lower-ranking suit in at the three-level. With 7-11 you do not plan on bidding again unless partner makes a forcing or invitational bid. With 15+ you are expected to bid again even if partner makes a minimum bid.

LHO	Partner	RHO	You
1♣	pass	pass	2♣

Here 2♣ shows the majors.

LHO	Partner	RHO	You
1♡	pass	pass	2♡

Here 2♡ shows five spades plus a five- or six-card minor.

420. Jump bids in the balancing seat are constructive, *not* weak. A jump in a suit shows a six-card suit with 12-15 HCP.

LHO	Partner	RHO	You
1♡	pass	pass	?

a) ♠ A Q J 8 7 6   ♡ A 5 4   ◊ K 4   ♣ 3 2
b) ♠ A Q J 8 7 6   ♡ J 5 4   ◊ 5 4 3   ♣ 2

With (a), bid 2♠. With (b), bid 1♠.

In direct seat, overcall 1♠ with (a) and jump to 2♠, weak, with (b).

421. When a 1♣ opening bid is passed to you, keep in mind partner was not strong enough to overcall a measly 1♣ bid.

422. When a 1♣ opening bid is passed to you, check your club length. If you are short, partner may yet have a good hand with strong clubs. If you have club length, chances are partner is weak.

LHO	Partner	RHO	You
1♣	pass	pass	?

a)   ♠Q4 ♡876 ◇KJ76 ♣AJ97
b)   ♠Q98 ♡A975 ◇KJ65 ♣74

With (a), pass. Given your club length, partner is probably short in clubs and must be quite weak not to be able to make a peep at the one-level. Opener probably has an 18-19 point balanced hand and is longing to get back into the bidding.

With (b), double. Your club shortness indicates partner may have a good hand with clubs after all.

423. When a minor-suit opening bid is passed to you, be careful about reopening when you have a singleton in either major, particularly spades. The next thing you know, the opponents will find their spade fit and you will be under the gun answering partner's questions.

LHO	Partner	RHO	You
1◇	pass	pass	?

♠4 ♡AJ87 ◇KJ43 ♣10987

Where are the spades? I'll let you in on a little secret; partner doesn't have them. Pass!

424. Reopening in the passout seat with a double jump to the three-level of a major suit shows an opening bid with a seven-card suit.

A jump from 1♣ to 3◇ suggests a solid suit.

LHO	Partner	RHO	You
1♣	pass	pass	?

a)   ♠A4 ♡QJ96542 ◇AJ9 ♣2
b)   ♠QJ3 ♡10 ◇AKQ9864 ♣J3

With (a), bid 3♡ to show this hand-type in the passout seat.

With (b), try 3◇ to show a likely seven-card solid suit.

425. And the best for last: The jump cuebid. The jump cuebid shows a solid suit (usually a minor) and asks partner to bid notrump with a stopper in the opponent's suit.

LHO	Partner	RHO	You
1♠	pass	pass	?

a)   ♠ 4 2   ♡ A 4   ◇ A K Q 10 8 7 6   ♣ 8 2

b)   ♠ K 4   ♡ A 4   ◇ A K Q 10 8 7 6   ♣ 8 2

With (a), bid 3♠. A good partner will have a spade stopper and bid 3NT. If not, convert any number of clubs partner bids to the same number of diamonds.

With (b), bid 3NT. No, this is not a misprint. You are *gambling*! Sometimes you have to. It's fun... when it works! If they run the clubs, blame it on me. Just don't look nervous! (You will anyway.)

WHEN THE OPPONENTS DIE OUT AT THE TWO-LEVEL

426. When the opponents give up the ship at the two-level, you and your partner usually have as many high-card points as they do — at worst, they will have 22 to your 18.

427. If the opponents have a known eight-card fit and you have a singleton in their suit, double with as little as 8 HCP; with a doubleton in their suit, reopen with 10+ HCP.

428. Thou shalt not let the opponents play in a contract of 2♥ or lower when they have a known eight-card fit (or longer) and you have shortness in their suit. The bad news is that they won't let *you* play in a contract of 2♥ or lower when you have an eight- or nine-card fit. You can bet on it.

429. Fact: If the opponents have an eight-card fit, your side also has an eight-card fit (or longer) about 85% of the time. If the opponents have a nine-card fit (or longer), your side will have at least an eight-card fit 100% of the time.

430. A reopening bid in a suit should be considered an attempt to push them up one level higher. With a good hand, you would have bid earlier.

LHO	Partner	RHO	You
		1♡	pass
2♡	pass	pass	?

♠ A 9 8 5 4   ♡ 5 4   ◇ K 5 4   ♣ 4 3 2

Bid 2♠. They have an eight-card fit and you have a five-card major. Don't sell out. A good partner will realize that you were not strong enough to overcall 1♠.

431. A reopening bid of 2NT after the opponents have found a major-suit fit is a minor-suit takeout.

LHO	Partner	RHO	You
		1♡	pass
2♡	pass	pass	?

♠ 4   ♡ 4 3 2   ◇ K J 1 0 4   ♣ A J 9 7 6

Don't sell out! Bid 2NT for the minors.

432. A reopening bid of 2NT after the opponents have not found a fit is natural. It shows 13-15 HCP and is definitely risky. However, the good news is you won't get your winners ruffed away in a crossruff.

♠ A 7 6   ♡ A J 1 0   ◇ Q 1 0 7 6   ♣ Q 1 0 6

LHO	Partner	RHO	You
		1◇	pass
1♡	pass	2◇	pass
2♡	pass	pass	?

Try 2NT. Partner usually has a little something.

433. The real risk in reopening the bidding with a light hand is your partner. He invariably has 10-13 HCP and thinks he must tell you all about it. He forgets you are counting on him for that much. Such partners must be trained. Read on.

434. The strategy behind balancing is to push the opponents to the three-level. If you succeed, mission accomplished! You should not compete to the three-level in your balancing partner's suit unless you have primary support, a side-suit singleton (or two side-suit doubletons) and 12-15 support points.

LHO	Partner	RHO	You
1♡	pass	2♡	pass
pass	2♠	3♡	?

a) ♠ A 10 4 ♡ 3 2 ◇ K J 8 7 ♣ Q J 3 2

b) ♠ A 10 4 2 ♡ 5 3 2 ◇ Q J 8 ♣ A 7 5

c) ♠ A 10 4 2 ♡ 3 ◇ K Q 9 8 7 ♣ 5 4 3

With (a) and (b), pass, partner is expecting this much.

With (c), you have a no-brainer 3♠ bid.

REDOUBLES

435. When a one- or two-level takeout double made by your *left*-hand opponent has been converted to penalties, 'redouble' by either player is a cry for help.

LHO	Partner	RHO	You
			1◇
dbl	pass	pass	?

♠ A Q 4   ♡ A K 3   ◇ 8 7 6 5   ♣ 9 8 7

RHO's pass has announced strong diamonds. Unless you are a masochist of the highest order, redouble for rescue.

436. A redouble of a takeout double made by your *right*-hand opponent shows extras and is not a cry for help.

LHO	Partner	RHO	You
			1◇
pass	pass	dbl	?

♠ A J 4   ♡ 6 5   ◇ A K J 9 7   ♣ A Q 9

You should redouble to show 18+ HCP. The redouble invites partner to come back to the party. In addition, the redouble in this sequence suggests a five-card suit, making it easier for partner to compete with three diamonds. With 18-19 balanced, bid 1NT instead of redoubling.

437. These same principles apply to overcalls that have been doubled for takeout and left in for penalties.

LHO	Partner	RHO	You
1♡	1♠	pass	pass
dbl	pass	pass	?

♠ — ♡ 10 8 6 ◇ Q 10 9 7 6 ♣ J 10 8 7 6

With RHO passing to announce strong spades, 1♠ doubled does not look healthy. Redouble to ask partner to choose an unbid suit.

LHO	Partner	RHO	You
		1♡	1♠
pass	pass	dbl	?

♠ A K Q 10 7 5 ♡ A J 9 ◇ 3 ♣ 10 9 8

Redouble here announces a powerful one-suited overcall. See Tip 436.

*438. A pass after RHO redoubles varies in meaning with the level of the auction.

LHO	Partner	RHO	You
1♡	dbl	redbl	?

In this, the most common redouble sequence of all, a pass by you is non-committal, telling partner to bail himself out if necessary. It says nothing about hearts.

LHO	Partner	RHO	You
3♡	dbl	redbl	pass

After an opening preempt, followed by a takeout double and a redouble, 'pass' is to play — presumably with something good in hearts. Some play that a pass is *always* non-committal after a redouble.

439. After you open the bidding and your LHO doubles and partner re-doubles, any subsequent double by either you or your partner is a penalty double — even at the one-level.

LHO	Partner	RHO	You
			1◇
dbl	redbl	pass	pass
1♡	pass	pass	?

♠ A 5 4   ♡ Q 10 9 7   ◇ A K 4 3 2   ♣ 2

Double. After a redouble by partner, tend to double any enemy runout with four cards in their suit.

°440. When your *right*-hand opponent makes a strength-showing redouble after having opened the bidding, 'pass' by you is a penalty pass.

LHO	Partner	RHO	You
		1♡	pass
pass	dbl	redbl	?

a)   ♠ K 5 4   ♡ 8 7 6 5   ◇ Q J 4   ♣ J 8 7
b)   ♠ A 2   ♡ K J 9 8 7   ◇ A 10 8 7   ♣ 10 9

With (a), bid 1♠. You do not wish to defend 1♡ redoubled.
    With (b), pass. You would love to defend 1♡ redoubled.

WHEN PARTNER OPENS AND SECOND HAND DOUBLES

*441. A new suit at the one-level is unlimited and forcing. It's as if the double never happened.

LHO	Partner	RHO	You
	1♣	dbl	?

♠ 4 ♡ A J 10 6 5 ◇ K J 5 4 3 ♣ Q 3

Bid 1♡. With a five-card major or a two-suited hand that can start with a one-level response, start bidding your suit(s). Do not redouble.

442. A two-level response denies the strength of a redouble.

LHO	Partner	RHO	You
	1♡	dbl	?

a) ♠ 5 4 3 ♡ 2 ◇ K Q J 8 7 6 ♣ 10 8 7
b) ♠ 5 4 3 ♡ 2 ◇ K Q J 8 7 6 ♣ A Q 8

With (a), bid 2◇, not forcing.
    With (b), redouble and then bid diamonds.

443. Most redoubles show balanced, or semi-balanced, hands with 11+ HCP plus some hope of doubling the opponents at a low level.

LHO	Partner	RHO	You
	1♣	dbl	?

a) ♠ A K 8 7 ♡ 4 3 ◇ 5 4 3 ♣ K J 5 4
b) ♠ K J 5 4 ♡ A Q 8 7 3 ◇ 5 ♣ J 7 6
c) ♠ K J 9 4 ♡ A Q 9 3 ◇ J 10 7 6 ♣ 9

With (a), bid 1♠. This is not a hand where you are looking to penalize them with a low-level penalty double when you have a fit with partner's suit. This is a hand where you want to show partner spades and clubs. Your 1♠ response is unlimited and forcing.

With (b), bid 1♡. The opponents surely have a home in diamonds. Better to look for your own best contract before the diamond preempts start.

With (c), redouble. This is a defensive hand. The opponents may not have a home.

*444. With three-card support for partner's major-suit opening, raise to two with 5-8 HCP, pass with 9-10 HCP and redouble with 11+ HCP.

LHO	Partner	RHO	You
	1♠	dbl	?

a) ♠A 8 7 ♡5 4 ◇J 10 8 7 ♣J 5 4 3
b) ♠A 8 7 ♡5 4 ◇K Q 8 7 ♣Q 10 8 7
c) ♠A 8 7 ♡5 4 ◇A J 5 4 ♣5 4 3 2

With (a), bid 2♠ (5-8 HCP).

With (b), redouble and then bid a minimum number of spades (11-12 HCP).

With (c), with 9-10 HCP and three-card major-suit support, pass and then support partner at your first opportunity. (You should jump in partner's suit if he bids in front of you showing extra strength. After all he doesn't know that you have a pretty good hand.) This is not a mainstream approach, but it works because it reduces the range of a direct raise to the two-level.

If you adopt this tip, you will be involved in sequences like this with 9-10 HCP and three-card support:

LHO	Partner	RHO	You
	1♠	dbl	pass
2♡	pass	pass	2♠

This sequence shows a stronger hand than a direct raise to 2♠ but not quite strong enough to redouble.

LHO	Partner	RHO	You
	1♠	dbl	pass
2♣	2♡	pass	?

Bid 3♠. Partner has bid in front of you so jump to show 9-10 HCP.

*445. With primary support for partner's major, you have many ways to raise.

LHO	Partner	RHO	You
	1♠	dbl	?

a) ♠Q J 5 4 ♡8 7 6 ◇K 8 7 ♣8 7 6
b) ♠Q 10 8 7 ♡4 ◇Q 9 7 5 ♣8 7 4 2
c) ♠J 9 7 6 5 ♡3 ◇K 8 7 6 5 ♣4 2
d) ♠A Q 8 7 ♡5 4 ◇K J 4 3 ♣8 7 6
e) ♠A Q 8 7 ♡5 4 ◇K J 5 4 ♣Q 4 3
f) ♠A Q 7 6 ♡A 4 ◇K Q 8 7 ♣8 7 6

With (a), bid 2♠, weak.

With (b), bid 3♠, preemptive.

With (c), bid 4♠, more preemptive and more distributional. A weak freak.

With (d), bid 2NT, conventional, showing 10-11 support points. The equivalent of a limit raise.

With (e), bid 3NT, 12-14 support points, equal to a forcing raise.

With (f), redouble, and then jump to 4♠ (15-16 support points).

446. Any jump bid is preemptive.

LHO	Partner	RHO	You
	1◇	dbl	?

♠K J 10 8 7 6 ♡4 ◇J 10 8 ♣10 8 7

Bid 2♠ to show a reasonable six-card suit with 5-7 HCP. With stronger hands bid 1♠, unlimited and forcing. When the bid to your right is strong (RHO's double), a jump by you is preemptive.

447. Redouble *promises* another bid if partner passes.

LHO	Partner	RHO	You
	1♠	dbl	redbl
2♣	pass	pass	?

♠ K 4   ♡ A 9 8 7   ◇ Q J 8 7   ♣ J 8 7

Whatever you do, don't pass! Partner can have a whale of a hand. Divorces have resulted from 2♣ being passed out. (Just kidding, only separations.)

Are you're wondering what I would bid? Well I'm not thrilled with my choice but I'd stick a club in with my spades and bid 2♠. I consider this the lesser of evils. 'Double' would be for penalty after partner redoubles and the clubs should be stronger. 2NT would show a club stopper, 2◇ and 2♡ suggest five-card suits, particularly 2♡, and both are unlimited and forcing. To me, 2♠ is the lesser evil. Oh yes, whenever one does something like this, one must complain about the lighting when partner starts asking embarrassing questions.

TWO-SUITED OVERCALLS

448. After a 1♣ or 1◊ opening bid, a cuebid of 2♣ or 2◊ (**Michaels cuebid**) shows 5-5 or 6-5 in the majors with 7-11 HCP. With 12-14 HCP, a 'tweener', overcall 1♠ and then bid hearts at the two-level or the three-level. With 15+ 'working' HCP, (no jacks or queens in the short suits), cuebid and bid again after partner makes a minimum response.

LHO	Partner	RHO	You
		1◊	?

a) ♠ A Q 8 7 6 ♡ K 10 9 5 4 ◊ 4 ♣ 5 4
b) ♠ A K J 8 7 ♡ K J 9 8 7 ◊ 3 ♣ 3 2
c) ♠ A K J 8 7 ♡ A K J 9 5 ◊ 4 ♣ 10 8

With (a), bid 2◊. You are near the top of the minimum range.

With (b), bid 1♠. You have a 'tweener', 12-14 HCP.

With (c), bid 2◊ and bid again after partner responds — 17 revalued points. (Concentrated strength in the two long suits is worth at *least* 1 extra point.)

*449. After a 1♡ or 1♠ opening bid, a cuebid of 2♡ or 2♠ shows five cards in the other major plus five or six cards in an unspecified minor (Michaels cuebid), and either 8-11 HCP or 16+ HCP. With 12-15 HCP, another 'tweener', overcall 1♠ and bid the minor next. (See Tip 100.)

LHO	Partner	RHO	You
		1♡	?

a) ♠ A 10 9 5 4 ♡ 4 ◊ 4 3 ♣ K Q J 8 7
b) ♠ A Q 9 8 7 ♡ 5 ◊ 4 3 ♣ A Q 10 8 7
c) ♠ A K J 9 7 ♡ 4 ◊ K 4 ♣ K Q J 6 5

With (a), bid 2♡.

With (b), bid 1♠ — too strong to bid 2♡. And don't forget the upgrade with the concentrated strength in the two long suits.

With (c), bid 2♡ and bid again after partner responds. This hand should be upgraded because of the trick-taking power of the two long suits — plus the ◇K should be a trick in back of the opening bidder who figures to have the ace if partner doesn't.

450. After a 1♡ or 1♠ opening, a direct overcall of 2NT shows the minors (either 5-5 or 6-5) with 8-11 HCP or 16+ HCP. With 12-15 HCP, overcall in diamonds and bid clubs later if feasible.

LHO	Partner	RHO	You
		1♠	?

a) ♠5 ♡K4 ◇AJ1098 ♣QJ876
b) ♠5 ♡K4 ◇AQJ98 ♣QJ1087
c) ♠5 ♡K4 ◇AKJ98 ♣AQ1087

With (a), bid 2NT. With (b), bid 2◇ — too strong to bid 2NT and hope to get clubs in at the three-level. You guessed it, another 'tweener'.

With (c), bid 2NT and then bid again after partner makes a minimum response.

Two-suited cuebids that force partner to the three-level to respond require slightly stronger ranges. These ranges are 8-11, 16+ for the cuebid and 12-15 for the 'tweeners'.

451. After a two-suited cuebid, the bidding may continue in such a way that partner does not respond. For example, your left-hand opponent may bid. If the bidding comes back to you dead, pass with the 8-11 point hand, double with the stronger hand.

LHO	Partner	RHO	You
		1♠	2NT
3♠	pass	pass	

a) ♠4 ♡K4 ◇AJ1098 ♣QJ987
b) ♠3 ♡K4 ◇AQ1098 ♣AKJ65

With (a), pass.

With (b), double to show a powerful two-suiter.

REVIEW OF TWO-SUITED OVERCALLS

Two-suited overcalls that show both majors or both minors are assumed to have 5-5 or 6-5 distribution either way. Two-suited overcalls that show a major and a minor are assumed to have 5-5 or 5-6 distribution with five cards in the major and five or six in the minor, not vice versa. Vulnerability plus strong intermediates in at least one of the suits, particularly with a minimum point count, must be a major consideration. Amen.

THE WEAK TWO-BID

452. Think of a weak two as an opening three-bid with one fewer card.

    a)   ♠ 8 7 ♡ A Q 10 9 7 6 2 ◇ J 5 4 ♣ 7

    b)   ♠ 8 7 ♡ A Q 10 9 7 6 ◇ J 5 4 ♣ 7 6

With (a), open 3♡.

    With (b), open 2♡.

453. There is no such animal as a Weak Two in clubs. A 2♣ opening bid is reserved for all game-going suit-oriented hands as well as balanced hands in the 22-24 or 27-28 HCP range.

    a)   ♠ A K J 10 8 7 ♡ A K 4 ◇ A Q J ♣ 5

    b)   ♠ K Q 4 ♡ A K 6 5 ◇ A K 5 4 ♣ K 2

Open 2♣ on both of these hands. With (a), rebid 2♠.

    With (b), rebid 2NT showing 22-24 HCP.

454. When you play Weak Twos, the 2NT opening bid shows 20-21 (or a flawed 22). A flawed 22 might have a doubleton KQ, KJ or QJ or any 4-3-3-3 pattern with no strong interior spot cards.

    a)   ♠ A J 8 ♡ K Q 4 3 ◇ A K 4 ♣ A 5 4

    b)   ♠ Q J ♡ A K J 2 ◇ K Q 3 2 ♣ K Q J

Open both hands 2NT. Hand (b) is a flawed 22.

*455. If you are lucky enough to be gazing at stronger balanced hands, open 3NT with 25-26; open 2♣ and rebid 3NT with 27-28 HCP.

    a)   ♠ A K 4 ♡ K Q 8 7 ◇ A J ♣ A K J 4

    b)   ♠ A K J ♡ A K J 4 ◇ A J 8 ♣ A Q 5

With (a), open 3NT.

With (b), open 2♣ and rebid 3NT.

Some play that an opening bid of 3NT shows a solid seven- or eight-card minor with no outside stoppers (**Gambling 3NT**). Others use the bid to show a solid minor suit (six or seven cards) with stoppers in at least two other suits (**Strong Gambling 3NT**). These players never get 27-28 point hands so they don't think they are giving up too much.

456. 2◇ is an optional Weak Two. Some players use an opening 2◇ bid to show other types of hand — Multi, Flannery, Roman, etc. Explanations are in the section on Conventions (Tips 480-497).

457. Most Weak Two-bids fall into the 6-9 HCP range; more important is the strength of the suit. Vulnerable, the suit should have three of the top five honor cards or two of the top five honors with the 9 and 8 thrown in for good measure.

a) ♠ K J 8 6 4 2 ♡ K 4 ◇ 7 6 2 ♣ 4 2
b) ♠ K Q 10 7 6 3 ♡ K 4 ◇ 7 6 2 ♣ 4 2
c) ♠ Q 10 7 6 5 2 ♡ 4 3 ◇ A J 6 ♣ 6 4
d) ♠ Q J 9 8 4 3 ♡ 4 3 ◇ A J 5 ♣ 6 5

With (a), open 2♠ not vulnerable, pass vulnerable.

With (b), open 2♠ at any vulnerability.

With (c), open 2♠ not vulnerable, pass vulnerable.

With (d), open 2♠ at any vulnerability.

458. *Third seat* Weak Two-bids can be opened with strong five-card suits. Partner is a passed hand and must be trained not to tamper with third seat Weak Twos.

LHO	Partner	RHO	You
	pass	pass	?

♠ 4 3 ♡ K Q J 10 4 ◇ K 4 3 ♣ 9 8 7

Open 2♡ and join the world of thieves.

459. Fourth-seat Weak Twos, like *all* fourth seat preempts, show hands that are as close to an opening one-bid as possible. The range is 10-12 HCP.

LHO	Partner	RHO	You
pass	pass	pass	?

♠ A K 10 5 4 3   ♡ 5 4   ◇ Q J 4   ♣ J 5

Open 2♠. Partner will play you for something like this in fourth seat.

460. Do not open a Weak Two with a void. Partner assumes a one-suited hand, and you may lose a fit in another suit.

♠ —   ♡ A J 8 7 6 5   ◇ K 4 3 2   ♣ J 5 4

Pass; it is anti-percentage to open 2♡.

461. Do not open a Weak Two in one major with four cards in the other major — unless your six-card major is independent and can play opposite a singleton easily. Do not open 2◇, weak, with a side four-card major.

a) ♠ A 10 4 3   ♡ A 10 8 4 3 2   ◇ 2   ♣ 9 8
b) ♠ Q 7 6 5   ♡ K Q J 10 8 7   ◇ 4 3   ♣ 10

With (a), pass. If you open 2♡, you might miss a better fit in spades.

With (b), open 2♡. Your hearts are so good that it won't matter if you miss a fit in spades.

462. Do not open a Weak Two with a side five-card suit.

1) You may miss a better fit in your second suit.
2) Partner will not be expecting a side five-card suit.

You hold:

♠ 4   ♡ A 10 8 7 6 5   ◇ K 10 8 7 6   ♣ 3

Pass; do not open this hand. Your turn will come.

*463. It is permissible to open a *vulnerable* Weak Two with a solid six-card suit, 6-3-2-2 distribution, and not so much as a jack on the side. Not vulnerable, partner will never play you for such a strong hand.

♠ A K Q J 5 4   ♡ 5 4   ◇ 6 5 4   ♣ 3 2

Vulnerable, open 2♠. Not vulnerable, open 1♠ or pass depending upon partnership agreement.

464. It is permissible to open a Weak Two with a side four-card minor.

♠ A J 10 5 4 3   ♡ 3   ◇ Q 10 9 8   ♣ 3 2

Open 2♠ at any vulnerability.

465. In a competitive auction, the Weak Two-bidder does not take the sacrifice. If a sacrifice is to be taken, it is his partner who takes it. Reread this one.

Not vul. vs. vul.

LHO	Partner	RHO	You
			2♡
2♠	4♡	4♠	?

♠ 5   ♡ K Q J 10 4 3   ◇ Q 7 6 5   ♣ 3 2

Pass. Partner knows the vulnerability and also knows more about your hand than vice versa.

*466. If partner responds 2NT, forcing, partner asks you to describe your hand further. You have some options. You can:

(i) Rebid your suit with a minimum.
(ii) Raise to 3NT with a solid, or near solid, suit, i.e., AKJxxx.
(iii) Show a side ace or king (a 'feature') with a maximum.
(iv) Jump to the four-level in a strong four-card minor — if you have one.
(v) Jump to game with a strong suit plus a maximum plus a singleton.

In fact, there are many (too many to list) other methods of responding to Weak Twos.

LHO	Partner	RHO	You
			2♠
pass	2NT	pass	?

a) ♠ Q J 10 5 4 3 ♡ 4 2 ◇ A J 10 ♣ 8 7
b) ♠ Q J 10 5 4 3 ♡ 4 2 ◇ K 7 6 ♣ 8 7
c) ♠ A K J 10 8 7 ♡ 2 ◇ 7 6 5 4 ♣ J 3
d) ♠ A 10 9 8 7 6 ♡ 10 8 ◇ K J 10 4 ♣ 3
e) ♠ K Q 9 8 7 5 ♡ 10 ◇ J 8 7 6 ♣ 4 3
f) ♠ A K J 9 7 6 ♡ 4 3 ◇ 8 7 6 ♣ 3 2

With (a), bid 3◇. Show the feature with a near maximum.

With (b), bid 3♠. No feature-showing with minimums.

With (c), bid 4♠. Good suit with unbalanced distribution.

With (d), bid 4◇, showing a strong four-card minor with a maximum.

With (e), bid 3♠. This is a minimum Weak Two.

With (f), raise to 3NT. You have a notrump spade suit.

It should be noted that some play that a 2NT response asks for a singleton; others, that it asks for the range of the hand in both high-card points and suit strength by steps.

WHEN RESPONDING TO A WEAK TWO-BID

467. You are facing a weak hand. Lacking support, you should be looking at 16 or more HCP to try for game. With a strong side suit, 15 HCP will do. Remember, partner has a likely 7-8 HCP.

LHO	Partner	RHO	You
	2♠	pass	?

a)   ♠2 ♡AK543 ◊KQ87 ♣QJ3
b)   ♠2 ♡AQJ987 ◊AK3 ♣J10 5

With (a), pass. You don't have quite enough. That singleton spade is a downer. What suit will you set up for tricks?

With (b), bid 3♡, forcing.

468. Assuming you have a strong hand without a long suit of your own, the easiest way to find out about partner's hand is to make a forcing 2NT response. With a long suit and a strong hand, bid your suit — see (b) in previous tip.

LHO	Partner	RHO	You
	2♠	pass	?

a)   ♠87 ♡A987 ◊A87 ♣AK54
b)   ♠K4 ♡AK87 ◊AK432 ♣87

With (a), bid 2NT. If partner shows you a minimum, give up on game. If partner shows a feature bid 4♠. If partner bids 3NT, pass.

With (b), bid 4♠. This time you have enough opposite a minimum without needing to ask.

469. A leap to 3NT ends the auction. Partner is not allowed to bid again.

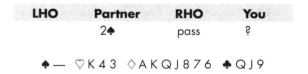

LHO	Partner	RHO	You
	2♠	pass	?

♠ — ♡ K 4 3 ◇ A K Q J 8 7 6 ♣ Q J 9

Bid 3NT and end the auction. If you want to give partner a choice between 3NT and four of partner's major, bid 2NT and then 3NT.

470. A single raise is weak — just a noise with three-card support to make life difficult for the opponents. Partner is not allowed to bid again or even think about bidding again!

LHO	Partner	RHO	You
	2♠	pass	?

♠ Q 4 3 ♡ 4 3 ◇ K Q 8 7 ♣ 10 9 8 7

Raise to 3♠. Make life miserable for them by upping the ante.

471. A double raise to game is a two-edged sword. It can be preemptive, or it can be made on a powerful hand that knows slam is out of the question.

LHO	Partner	RHO	You
	2♡	pass	?

a) ♠ 9 ♡ K 8 7 6 ◇ K 8 7 6 5 ♣ 10 8 7
b) ♠ A J 9 8 ♡ 10 5 ◇ A K ♣ A 9 8 7 6

Bid 4♡ with either hand. Let them worry about which hand type you have.

472. If you are incapable of passing 13-14 point hands with a singleton in partner's suit and no long suit of your own, do not play Weak Two-bids!

LHO	Partner	RHO	You
	2♠	pass	?

♠ 3 ♡ A J 8 7 ◇ K Q 8 7 ♣ K J 4 3

Pass with the speed of summer lightning!

WHEN THEY OPEN A WEAK TWO

473. Treat a Weak Two opening as a one-bid. If you would double one of the suit being opened, double the Weak Two-bid as well.

LHO	Partner	RHO	You
		2♡	?

♠A765 ♡54 ◇AK5 ♣J1087

You would double 1♡, so double 2♡.

474. If you would have overcalled an opening one-bid with 1NT showing 15-18 HCP, overcall a Weak Two opening with 2NT, showing 16-19 HCP or 15 HCP and super strong intermediates.

LHO	Partner	RHO	You
		2♡	?

♠AQ4 ♡KJ4 ◇QJ9 ♣AJ93

Bid 2NT.

475. To overcall at the two-level, you need either a strong five-card suit with 12-16 HCP or a reasonable six-card suit with 11-15 HCP. A three-level overcall shows a strong six-card suit with opening bid values.

LHO	Partner	RHO	You
		2♡	?

a) ♠KJ543 ♡A54 ◇J5 ♣A76
b) ♠KJ1042 ♡A76 ◇54 ♣A76
c) ♠K109432 ♡AJ4 ◇K4 ♣65
d) ♠54 ♡A87 ◇Q3 ♣KQ5432

With (a), pass. Those spade spots plus the death distribution (5-3-3-2) make a two-level overcall far too risky.

With (b), overcall 2♠ — you have suit 'texture'.

With (c), overcall 2♠ — never discount the advantage of that sixth card in your long suit. And that K109 combination is not chopped liver either.

With (d), pass — no intermediates in your long suit and too many side suit losers.

*476. You can cuebid their suit to ask for a stopper in their suit. The cuebid shows a solid minor, presumably with stoppers in the other suits.

LHO	Partner	RHO	You
		2♡	?

♠ K 4   ♡ 5 4   ◇ A 3   ♣ A K Q 6 5 4 3

Bid 3♡, asking partner to bid 3NT with a heart stopper.

LHO	Partner	RHO	You
		2♠	?

♠ K 4   ♡ 5 4   ◇ A 3   ♣ A K Q 6 5 4 3

Bid 3NT. No second choice.

*477. A jump to the four-level in a minor shows five or six cards in the minor and exactly five cards in the unbid major. Partner needs next to nothing to bid game in one of your suits. This jump is not forcing, but partner should not pass with a trick for you. It is called **Leaping Michaels**.

LHO	Partner	RHO	You
		2♡	?

♠ A Q 10 5 4   ♡ 2   ◇ A K J 4 3 2   ♣ 2

Leap to 4◇, showing a diamond-spade hand needing oh so little for game. Three spades headed by the jack could easily be enough!

478. With five or six cards in their suit, pass and hope partner can reopen with a double.

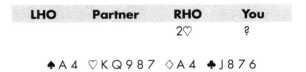

LHO	Partner	RHO	You
		2♡	?

♠A4 ♡KQ987 ◇A4 ♣J876

Pass — patience, patience, patience. The other day I was planning to open 2♠ holding

♠AJ10632 ♡KQ ◇102 ♣1043

when lo and behold my right hand opponent opened 2♠! I checked the backs of my cards and passed, next hand passed, and my partner reopened with a takeout double. I passed and we beat it two tricks. I led the ♡K, but the ◇10 was the killing lead.

*479. With most minor two-suiters, bid 3◇ and then bid clubs. However, with an exceptionally powerful minor two-suiter that wishes to play game regardless, make a jump cuebid.

LHO	Partner	RHO	You
		2♠	?

a) ♠3 ♡65 ◇AQJ87 ♣AQ1098
b) ♠— ♡4 ◇AQ10643 ♣AK10876

With (a), bid 3◇ and hope to bid clubs later.

   With (b), bid 4♠. Use the jump cuebid to describe a powerful minor two-suiter with slam possibilities. (This was an idea that came from the late Paul Soloway.) A direct jump to 4NT describes a more modest two-suiter, usually 6-5 or 5-6. However, this jump is stronger than hand (a), but weaker than hand (b).

CONVENTIONS TO BE FAMILIAR WITH

480. **The Weak Jump Overcall**: The weak jump overcall shows the same type of hand as a weak two-bid.

LHO	Partner	RHO	You
		1♡	?

♠ K Q 10 8 7 6   ♡ 4   ◇ Q J 4   ♣ 4 3 2

Bid 2♠. You would open this hand 2♠, so make a weak jump overcall with it.

481. Responses to a two-level weak jump overcall are the same as responses to a weak two-bid.

482. **Flannery 2◇**: An opening bid of 2◇ that shows five hearts, four spades and 11-15 HCP. With a stronger hand, open 1♡ and reverse into spades.

483. **Multi 2◇**: Another 2◇ opening bid showing a weak two-bid in an unspecified major. Other possible meanings can be tagged on to the bid depending on what the 2◇ opener rebids.

484. **Roman 2◇**: An opening 2◇ bid that shows a strong hand with any 5-4-4-0 or 4-4-4-1 distribution with a range of 17-20 HCP. A 2NT response is positive asking opener to bid his short suit.

*485. **Drury:** An artificial passed-hand response of 2♣ to an opening bid of 1♡ or 1♠ with three- or four-card support. It asks the opener whether he has a real opening bid or has opened light to steal a partscore. Nine times out of ten, the Drury bidder has 10-11 HCP with three-card support. Passing 2♣ and then doubling 2♠, if it comes around to you, is a takeout double of spades.

LHO	Partner	RHO	You
			pass
pass	1♠	pass	?

♠ A 8 7 ♡ K 3 ◇ A 7 6 5 ♣ 7 6 5 4

Playing Drury, respond 2♣. In one of the popular sets of responses to Drury, opener rebids the original suit with less than a full opening bid and 2◇ with a full opening bid or better. Jumps by the opener have specific meanings. If opener bids 2◇, responder bids 2♠ with three spades and 3♠ with four spades. Neither bid is forcing.

486. If the opponents use Drury, double 2♣ to show strong clubs. It is a lead directing double.

487. **The Responsive Double:** After partner makes a takeout double of a major-suit opening bid and third hand raises opener's suit to the two- or three-level, double by you either shows a balanced hand or length in both minors. It is *not* a penalty double. The usual range is 7-11 HCP depending upon the level of the raise.

LHO	Partner	RHO	You
1♡	dbl	2♡	?

a) ♠ A J 7 ♡ 5 4 3 2 ◇ K 8 7 ♣ Q 8 7
b) ♠ A 8 ♡ 9 7 3 ◇ J 10 8 4 ♣ K 4 3 2

With (a), double to show high-card strength *without* a long suit.
With (b), double. This time you do have two places to play.

488. When both majors are unbid, a responsive double shows equal length in the majors, either three or four. With four cards in one major and three in the other, bid the four-card major.

LHO	Partner	RHO	You
1◇	dbl	2◇	?

a) ♠K54 ♡A54 ◇8765 ♣J87
b) ♠QJ54 ♡K543 ◇54 ♣J87
c) ♠QJ54 ♡K53 ◇54 ♣J874

Double on (a) and (b). You have equal length in the unbid majors.
　　With (c), bid 2♠.

*489. When one major suit is unbid, a responsive double leans toward the minors. If a responsive double is made with a four-card major (rare), the doubler is intending to bid the suit next to show 10-11 HCP.

LHO	Partner	RHO	You
1♠	dbl	2♠	?

a) ♠987 ♡43 ◇AJ54 ♣K1065
b) ♠43 ♡J1032 ◇Q32 ♣AK87
c) ♠43 ♡KJ98 ◇K54 ♣7432

With (a), double. Perfect. With (b), double and then bid hearts to show four hearts and a hand stronger than a direct 3♡ bid. (See next answer.)
　　With (c), bid 3♡ directly; weaker than doubling and then bidding 3♡.

490. **The Responsive Double after partner overcalls**: After partner overcalls and third hand raises below game, double by fourth hand is takeout for the other two suits, usually 5-5, conceivably 5-4 (the unbid major having five cards) with 8+ HCP.

LHO	Partner	RHO	You
1♣	1♡	2♣	?

a) ♠K7532 ♡5 ◇AJ1084 ♣32
b) ♠A9743 ♡92 ◇KQ75 ♣32
c) ♠K43 ♡2 ◇Q432 ♣KJ1087

With (a), double. With (b), double.
　　With (c), pass. When you play responsive doubles, you can't change systems in midstream and suddenly make a penalty double instead!

491. **Texas Transfers:** When partner opens 1NT and catches you with a six- or seven-card major and 6-10 HCP, a response of 4◇ is a transfer to 4♡ and a response of 4♡ is a transfer to 4♠. Now, partner, the stronger hand, is the declarer. This sequence is also a springboard to following up your transfer response by bidding 4NT, Roman Keycard Blackwood (RKCB) for your major. In this variation partner counts the agreed major-suit king as an ace and can even show you if he has the trump queen! See Tip 285.

LHO	Partner	RHO	You
	1NT	pass	?

a) ♠ A J 9 8 7 5 4   ♡ 4   ◇ 5 4 3   ♣ J 10
b) ♠ 5 4   ♡ K J 9 8 7 4 3   ◇ Q J 4   ♣ 3
c) ♠ 5   ♡ A Q J 10 5 3 2   ◇ K Q J   ♣ K J

With (a), respond 4♡ and pray your partner has not forgotten what you are playing and that it is a transfer to 4♠!

With (b), respond 4◇ and keep praying.

With (c), respond 4◇ and then bid 4NT, RKCB for hearts. Notice that you have one of the five possible keycards. If partner shows two keycards, settle for 5♡. If partner shows three, meaning an ace or the ♡K is missing, settle for 6♡. If partner shows four, meaning partner has the three missing aces as well as the ♡K, 'settle' for 7NT as you can count thirteen top tricks!

*492. **Five Ace Blackwood:** In this variation, the trump king is counted as an 'ace'. There are now five 'aces' in the deck! To bid a slam you need at least four of the five 'aces'. Responses to Five Ace Blackwood are:

5♣	1 or 4 aces
5◇	0 or 3 aces
5♡	2 aces
5♠	2 aces with extras

A response of five aces is so off the wall that it is not even mentioned. If your partner asks you for aces and you have five, bid ten notrump and expect to make overtricks!

LHO	Partner	RHO	You
	1♠	pass	2♡
pass	3♠	pass	4♠
pass	4NT	pass	?

♠ K 4   ♡ A J 10 4 3   ◇ K J 4   ♣ 4 3 2

The ♠K counts as an 'ace' so you have two 'aces'. Respond 5♡.

493. **Roman Keycard Blackwood:** The responder counts both the king and the queen of the agreed suit. In the version called '1430', the responses are:

5♣	1 or 4 keycards (14)
5◇	3 or 0 keycards (30)
5♡	2 without the queen
5♠	2 with the queen

For practical purposes, the responder will not have five keycards. So forget it.

The alternate set of responses is called 3014 — the first two responses are exchanged. These responses are:

5♣	3 or 0 keycards (30)
5◇	1 or 4 keycards (14)
5♡	2 without the queen
5♠	2 with the queen

Put me in the '1430' camp. I even wrote a book about it!

494. **Wolff Signoff:** This convention was designed by Bobby Wolff to allow the responder to be able to sign off in this and similar sequences:

Partner	You
1♣	1♡/1♠
2NT	3♣

The 3♣ bid is an artificial response asking opener to rebid 3◇ with a doubleton in your major or to bid three of your major with three-card support.

If opener bids 3◇, you can pass with a weak heart-diamond two-suiter, you can return to 3♡, a signoff, or you can bid 3NT, a mild slam try in clubs.

If opener bids three of your major, you can pass or perhaps bid four of your major knowing of three-card support.

495. **Jacoby 2NT Response**: A 2NT response to a major-suit opening bid showing a balanced game-forcing raise. With visions of slam, opener has several ways of making descriptive rebids. This response (if you decide to use it) replaces the former 2NT response that showed 13-15 HCP, balanced, with fewer than four cards in partner's major.

496. Defenses to a 1NT opening bid

(i) **Cappelletti/Hamilton**

dbl	penalty
2♣	any one-suited hand
2◇	majors
2♡	hearts and a minor
2♠	spades and a minor
2NT	minors

(ii) **DONT**

dbl	any one-suited hand
2♣	clubs and another suit
2◇	diamonds and a major
2♡	majors
2♠	natural (weaker than 'dbl' followed by 2♠)
2NT	minors

(iii) **Landy**

dbl	penalty
2♣	majors
2◇/2♡/2♠	natural
2NT	minors

497. **The Support Double:** Used only by the opener after partner responds 1♡ or 1♠ and the opponents interfere *below the two-level* of partner's suit. When this happens, 'double' by the opener shows three-card support for responder's major and is an unlimited bid. Raising responder's major suit to the two-level shows four-card support, a normal two-level raise. Passing shows fewer than three cards in responder's major with a minimum opening bid.

LHO	Partner	RHO	You
			1◇
pass	1♡	2♣	?

a) ♠A 2 ♡K 7 6 ◇A Q 7 6 5 ♣4 3 2
b) ♠A 2 ♡K 7 6 4 ◇A Q 7 6 5 ♣3 2
c) ♠4 ♡K 7 6 ◇A K J 8 7 ♣A J 9 2
d) ♠Q 10 8 7 ♡5 ◇A Q 8 3 ♣A Q 9 8

With (a), double (support double), showing three-card heart support, an unlimited bid. However, responder assumes you have a simple raise to 2♡ for the time being.

With (b), bid 2♡. The *direct raise* over interference shows four-card support and *is limited* to a minimum hand.

With (c), double and then bid 3♣ (if partner bids 2♡) to complete the picture of your hand. This sequence shows extras.

With (d), pass showing a minimum with fewer than three hearts. 'Double' would not be a penalty double, it would be a support double showing three hearts! Bidding 2♠ would be a reverse showing 17+ HCP, and bidding 2NT is the equivalent of a jump to 2NT after a 1♡ response showing 18-19 HCP.

If RHO makes a takeout double instead of an overcall, 'redouble' by you, called a **Support Redouble,** now shows three-card heart support and a raise shows four. If RHO overcalls 1NT, natural, double is for penalty and support doubles are off.

WHAT'S LEFT

498. Opponents who bid to the heavens vulnerable against not with limited high-card strength invariably have wild distribution.

499. With nine winners in your own hand, plus an independent major suit, bid game. Do not invite. A good partner will give you the tenth trick.

LHO	Partner	RHO	You
		1◇	dbl
pass	1♡	2♣	?

♠ A K Q J 8 7   ♡ K Q 10   ◇ A J 5   ♣ 7

Jump to 4♠. Do not invite with 3♠.

500. If you are playing bridge with your husband, your wife, or your significant other as your partner, I salute you.

501. A 4-4 trump fit usually plays at least one trick better than a 5-3 trump fit.

You
♠ A Q J 4
♡ A Q 10 5 4
◇ A 2
♣ A 2

Dummy
♠ K 10 7 6
♡ K J 9
◇ 5 4 3
♣ 5 4 3

In a contract of 6♠, say you get a club lead. One possibility for a twelfth trick is to give up a club and ruff a club in your hand. You can't make 6♡ with a crowbar.

502. A 4-4 trump fit usually plays at least one trick better than a notrump contract.

You		Dummy
♠ K J 10 9		♠ A Q 4 2
♡ A 8 7		♡ 4 3
♢ K J 10		♢ A Q 8 7
♣ K 8 7		♣ A 4 2

Here, 6♠ is ice cold. All you have to do is ruff a heart in dummy. The losing club goes on the fourth diamond. Meanwhile, 6NT has no play. Notice that there are 31 HCP between the two hands. With a 4-4 trump fit, 31 or 32 HCP between the two hands is usually enough to make slam. Of course, it helps to have a strong trump suit and side-suit controls.

503. Their bidding often gives you the key to partner's distribution. This, in turn, can make your own bidding more accurate.

LHO	Partner	RHO	You
			1♡
1♠	2♡	2♠	?

♠ 7 6 5 4   ♡ A K J 10 8   ♢ A Q 10   ♣ 3

It doesn't take Einstein to figure out that partner is short in spades. Your hand is better than it looks. Either make a game try with 3♢ or shoot for the moon and bid 4♡. With the expected spade lead, you should be able to trump at least two of your spades in dummy. Do not make the all-time wimp bid of 3♡, which bars partner. If you want to involve partner, you have to bid a new suit.

504. The right bid with one partner may well be the wrong bid with another. Reread this one.

505. If you find yourself losing your hair when partner plays the hand, bid notrump quickly.

506. Partner is more apt to stay the course knowing your distribution as opposed to your point count.

507. Give up on fancy bids with weak partners. They figure to backfire. Correction: They *will* backfire.

508. More points are lost through cowardice than bravery. It's a bidder's game.

509. There isn't room at the table for four good hands. If everyone is bidding rather strongly, someone is lying. Just hope it isn't your partner. Notice I didn't mention you!

510. The greatest show of willpower on earth is not to mention to partner an obvious error. Repeated demonstrations of this may qualify you for sainthood or ultimately ulcerhood.

511. If you really want to improve your bridge, play with and against good players. Too many things work against weak players. You cannot improve your game under those circumstances. And be sure to read good books, like this one, he said modestly.

512. When you and your partner adopt a convention, be prepared for interference and make sure you know how to handle it.

513. With a weak hand and a choice of bids, one limited and one unlimited, make the limited bid. This is a biggie.

LHO	Partner	RHO	You
	1♡	pass	?

♠ K Q 8 7 2   ♡ J 10 4   ◇ 3 2   ♣ J 10 4

Your choices are 1♠, unlimited, or 2♡, limited. Bid 2♡. If you respond 1♠ and partner rebids 2♣ or 2◇, now 2♡ by you strongly suggests a doubleton heart. In fact, it would be an exception to have three hearts.

514. With a new partner, the fewer conventions the better.

515. If your partner appears uncomfortable with a certain convention, don't play it. Chances are it won't come up anyway. And chances are if it does, he'll screw it up.

516. When you have a choice of sensible bids, make the one that pays off the most if it works.

517. System cannot replace judgement. Nothing can.

518. They say you can't have good sex with your partner after a bad game. Wanted to see if you were awake!

519. Let the opponents make 'genius' bids.

520. Do not bid a grand slam in notrump unless you can count thirteen tricks. Do not bid a suit grand slam unless you have the AKQ of trumps between the two hands or a ten-card trump fit missing the queen. Avoid grand slams on finesses! They only seem to work for your opponents.

521. Always consider what partner has *not* bid.

LHO	Partner	RHO	You
1♣	pass	2♣	?

Partner wasn't able to overcall 1◇, 1♡ or 1♠. Negative inferences abound during the bidding.

522. A partner who passes over an opposing opening bid and then comes to life later usually is well stacked in opener's first suit.

LHO	Partner	RHO	You
1♣	pass	pass	1♡
pass	2NT		

Partner has a strong hand with clubs, perhaps 16-17 HCP with short hearts, which is why he didn't overcall 1NT directly.

523. If partner says he enjoyed playing with you after you've had a bad game and appears to be telling the truth, this partner could be a 'keeper'.

524. Do not let bad results get to you — or worse, let partner see that they have got to you. Assume things will turn around; they usually do.

525. A simple 'Nice bid' to partner goes a long way in cementing a partnership.

526. If you don't want to get doubled, bid in a confident manner. The opponents will be impressed, and so will partner.

527. Don't be afraid to get into the bidding against experts. That's one reason why they win so often — opponents are beaten before they get to the table. Also, experts don't like defending against preempts any more than you do.

528. In most sequences, there is a captain and a private. The private is the first player to limit his hand. The troublesome sequences are the ones where neither hand is limited so there is no captain — or worse, there is one captain and one general!

529. As the auction continues, ask yourself what your partner already knows about your hand. Try not to tell the same story twice. In short, do not be a broken record.

530. It is easy to envision the perfect hand partner might have to make your overbidding look good. Partner never has that hand. Never.

531. If you are not playing with a strong player, avoid putting partner in what is likely to be a complicated contract. Give partner a little leeway. Partner will love you for it, and you'll live longer.

532. One of the great secrets to being a winning bridge player is knowing when to pass.

533. Susan Ross says that Tip 518 is a myth. She told me that her phone has been ringing off the hook ever since this book came out.

534. Half the blame for any misunderstanding can usually be placed on the partnership for failing to agree upon the meaning of simple bids. *Even a bad agreement is better than no agreement.*

535. It is better to agree on general principles than to discuss specific auctions — unless you intend to live two hundred years or so.

536. Unusual notrump bids, two-suited cuebids and two-suited overcalls (see tip #477) with an unspecified point-count range often lead to trouble, big trouble.

537. Avoid 'torture' auctions. Making two or three cuebids on the same hand is a sure way to drive partner over the edge.

538. When partner makes two or three bids, think not only in terms of partner's point-count, but equally important, partner's likely distribution.

539. To raise preemptive bids *without* trump support, count quick tricks, not points. To raise a vulnerable 3♡ or 3♠ bid to game, you need at *least* three quick tricks. To raise any other two- or three-level preempt to game, you need at *least* four quickies.

540. When partner opens the bidding and you have two sure defensive tricks outside of partner's suit, double any game contract they wind up in. You won't beat them all, but you'll beat most of them. See the next tip.

541. Don't expect to defeat every contract you double. If you do, you are not doubling enough.

542. Don't expect to make every slam you bid. If you do, you are not bidding enough slams.

543. Play with someone you like as a person and who likes you. Amen.

BONUS TIPS

544. Be aggressive in the bidding with fitting hands; be conservative with non-fitting hands.

545. Do not open the bidding with any hand that you would be ashamed to put down as dummy.

546. Count tricks when preempting. If you have the tricks, you don't need the points. But even if you have the points, you still need the tricks.

547. Bridge is a game of fits and misfits. You can take that statement any way you like.

548. Treat your partner as you would your best friend, you will be repaid in spades.

549. With five trumps headed by the ace or king plus a side-suit singleton, raise partner's one-level major-suit opening bid or overcall to game. Just do it!

550. With a minimum opening bid (11-15 HCP) that contains a singleton and no strong six-card suit or longer, pass if partner bids and rebids your singleton suit at the one- and two-levels.

551. Wild two-suited hands take truckloads of tricks **if** partner has a fit for one of the suits. If partner has a similar type hand with the two other suits, BEWARE. You are in the throes of a misfit. Don't get involved in a bidding war.

552. Playing a 15-17 notrump range, do not raise 1NT to 2NT with 8 HCP and 4-3-3-3 distribution. Playing a 16-18 notrump range, pass with 7 HCP and the same distribution.

553. When two misfitting hands with slam potential each have a six-card or longer suit, the player with strong intermediates in the long suit must take charge. If neither long suit has good intermediates, slam is going to be *very* 'iffy'. Very. It is usually best to settle for game.

554. To repeat: just pick out the tips that you and partner will be most comfortable with. You'll be happier, your partner will be happier, and I'll be happier.

Master Point Press on the Internet

www.masterpointpress.com
Our main site, with information about our books and software, reviews and more.

www.teachbridge.com
Our site for bridge teachers and students — free downloadable support material for our books, helpful articles and more.

www.bridgeblogging.com
Read and comment on regular articles from MPP authors and other bridge notables.

www.ebooksbridge.com
Purchase downloadable electronic versions of MPP books and software.